CENTAUR

The Metaphysics
of Leadership

CENTAUR
The Metaphysics of Leadership

SANDY COTTER

First published in 2020 by Centaur Leadership

Copyright © Sandy Cotter 2020

The moral right of Sandy Cotter to be identified as the author of this work has been asserted in accordance with the Copyright, Designs and Patents Act 1988.

All rights reserved. No part of this publication may be reproduced or transmitted in any form or by any means, electronic or mechanical including photocopying, recording or any information storage or retrieval system, without prior permission in writing from the publishers.

Every effort has been made to contact copyright holders. However, the publisher will be glad to rectify in future editions any inadvertent omissions brought to their attention.

ISBN 978-1-912892-44-0

Also available as an ebook
ISBN 978-1-912892-45-7

Typeset by Jill Sawyer
Cover design by Emma Ewbank
Printed and bound by CPI
Project management by whitefox

The Centaur Proposition: Three Offerings

A SEARCH FOR BURIED TREASURE

Would you like to know what unconscious attitudes keep you from expressing your full potential and learn how to access this lost resource? Classical depth psychology and latest brain research reveal that early life experiences etch attitudes into our *unconscious* mind that limit how we live. Centaur identifies these limiting attitudes and then provides a road map to self-achievement and actualization.

A TOTALLY ETHICAL UNFAIR ADVANTAGE

What would it be like to know how to motivate, influence or inspire another person within twenty seconds of meeting them? Through joint lenses of body-mind psychology and neuroscience, the Centaur model gives precisely this insight, which has been referred to as 'a totally ethical unfair advantage'.

A WAY TO MOVE THE WORLD IN A BETTER DIRECTION

Would you be interested in an idea of leadership rooted in ethical integrity? Philosophical psychologists, theoretical scientists along with philosophers and spiritual teachers across time suggest a deep organizing principle within nature – including human nature – that can guide us to 'elegance' and 'natural ethics'.

Contents

INTRODUCTION   1

CHAPTER ONE: AN INVITATION TO BE PSYCHOLOGICAL   21

    Freud and Neuroscience: An Unconscious Worldview Runs Your Life   21

    Reich's Body-Mind, Bioenergetics and Neuroscience   46

    Jung and Complexity Theory: An Organizing Principle Within   60

CHAPTER TWO: PRACTICAL APPLICATION   77

    Perspectives   77

    Three Basic Notions in Psychology   81

    The Character Continuum: Potential Not Pathology   83

    The Developmental Story   86

    Babyhood: The Crucible of Magicals and Romantics   86

    The Magicals: The Wizard and the Sprite   87

    The Romantics : The Poet and the Damsel   105

    Toddlerhood: The Crucible of Superheroes   123

    The Superheroes : The Wonder Woman and the Superman   124

    The 'Reason-able' Child: The Crucible of Guardians and Heroes   145

The Guardians: The Good Father and the Earth Mother	145
The Heroes : The Warrior and the Huntress	161

CHAPTER THREE: REFLECTIONS — 178

Faith in Current Times	179
William James and the Scientific Validation of the Human Spirit	187
What Can We Do?	193
In Summary and Conclusion	196

INTRODUCTION

This book is for the ethical men and women in the corporate community with whom I have worked for the last three decades. At the start of my career, the world of business could turn a blind eye to the importance of deeper reaches of morality and interpersonal respect, but since the world-changing impact of the 2008 financial crisis, philosophical topics like ethics and integrity have moved higher up the corporate agenda.

There are two original philosophical questions: 'What is there?' and 'What should we do?' In the realm of philosophy, the question 'What is there?' is called 'metaphysics' and the question 'What should we do?' is called 'ethics'. Applied personally, these questions become 'Who am I?' and 'How should I live with other people?'

These two questions inform this book and the answers I will be suggesting draw from my work with the Centaur model and the professional development of numerous corporate leaders over three decades.

Although these questions seem big, they have answers that are simple, positive and exquisitely human. Lately we have lost touch with this promising human simplicity and our world is the worse for it.

Events of recent decades highlight the seriousness of our situation: the near meltdown of the financial sector causing the worst recession in eighty years, the heartbreaking moral scandals of the systematic abuse of children in care and the radicalization of young minds from extremist dogma. And then, most recently, the rise of 'populism' in international politics. To my mind, these are signs of people not knowing who they are or how to live in the world with others.

Rediscovering the simple answers to the questions 'Who am I?' and 'How should I live with others?' offers a key to unlocking deeper potentials within us and provides a foundation for ethical and inspired living.

The Centaur approach, which is the basis of this book, examines the ideas of three grandfathers of psychological thought – Sigmund Freud, Wilhelm Reich and Carl Jung – creating a layered and nuanced picture of who we are as human beings. The model then goes on to make helpful links to the latest science of the brain that has revolutionized our understanding of human functioning over the past few decades.

Centaur unites psychological and philosophical thought from the past and scientific discoveries of the present. This fusion creates a spectacularly useful tool for leadership development and the creation of a positive, sustainable corporate culture.

Our introduction to the Centaur approach continues by posing the following question: Is everybody like me? The answer: No! and also Yes!

Most of us approach other people with the conscious or unconscious attitude 'Everybody is pretty much like me'. Within this frame of mind, we then treat everyone as we ourselves would like to be treated. As a result of this – *and often with the best will in the world* – we can make big mistakes in relating to others.

But questioning this orientation is difficult because at a profound (metaphysical) level the statement 'everybody is like me' is true and the (ethical) intention to treat others in ways we would wish for ourselves is valid. After all, the so-called 'Golden Rule' – 'Do unto others as you would have them do unto you' – is the relational basis of every major religion, most traditions of native wisdom and many well-regarded moral philosophies. (See opposite.)

Moreover, it is not only prophets and philosophers who think in these 'golden' terms. Some years ago a popular TV network challenged the nation to come up with a new and modern set of 'Ten Commandments'. People were asked to send in suggestions in their own words.

There was an enthusiastic response to this project that invited some deep thinking about how we live in the world together. Strikingly and remarkably, the choice for the number one spot – by a huge percentage – was 'Treat other people in ways you want to be treated yourself.'

Ancient Egypt: 'That which you hate to be done to you, do not to another.' From a Late-Period papyrus

Ancient India: '... by self-control and by making dharma (right conduct) your main focus, treat others as you treat yourself.' From the Hindu Mahabharata *Shanti Parva* l67:9

Ancient Greece: The Golden Rule was a common principle:

'Avoid doing what you would blame others for doing.' Thales

'Do not do to others that which angers you when they do it to you.' Isocrates

'What you do not want to happen to you, do not do it yourself either.' Sextus the Pythagorean

Ancient Persia: 'Whatever is disagreeable to yourself do not do unto others.' Pahlavi Texts of Zoroastrianism

Ancient Rome: 'Treat your inferior as you would wish your superior to treat you.' Seneca the Younger

Buddhism: 'Hurt not others in ways that you yourself would find hurtful.' Udanavarga 5:18

Sikhism: 'Precious like jewels are the minds of all. To hurt them is not at all good. If thou desirest thy Beloved, then hurt thou not anyone's heart.' Guru Arjan Dev Ji 259, Guru Granth Sahib

Jainism: 'A man should wander about treating all creatures as he himself would be treated.' Sutrakritanga, 1.11.33

Confucianism: 'How about "shu" [reciprocity]: never impose on others what you would not choose for yourself.' Confucius, Analects XV.24.

Taoism: 'Regard your neighbour's gain as your own gain, and your neighbour's loss as your own loss.' T'ai Shang Kan Ying P'ien

> **Judaism:** 'What is hateful to you, do not do to your fellow; this is the whole of the Torah; the rest is the explanation.' Hillel the Elder, Shabbath folio: 31a, Babylonian Talmud
>
> **Christianity:** 'Do to others what you would want them to do to you.' Jesus, Luke 6:31
>
> **Islam:** 'As you would have people do to you, do to them; and what you dislike to be done to you, don't do to them.' Muhammad, Kitab al-Kafi, vol.2, p.146
>
> **Bahaism:** 'And if thine eyes be turned towards justice, choose thou for thy neighbour that which thou choosest for thyself.' Baha'u'llah

Now, if this idea of treating others as we would like to be treated has been so deeply inscribed in human philosophy and belief over the ages *and if* it is what modern people consciously think of when asked to have an idea of right behaviour, *then why* does the attitude, 'Everybody is pretty much like me' often get us into trouble with other people?

The key to the conundrum is in imagining levels and layers when thinking about yourself and other people. The Centaur Approach charts two levels of human being: a surface personality where we can differ greatly from one another and an essential core which is the same in all of us.

At our deepest level of consciousness, the Golden Rule is a sterling guide, while at the level of everyday living it creates disaster after disaster.

An easy way to understand these levels is to think of the construction of our physical bodies. On the surface we differ remarkably from one another in size, proportion, colouring and facial features. It is easy to tell one of us from another by physical characteristics that are unique to each of us. The way we appear physically in the world in our very own way is equivalent to the level of our 'personality' self in the domain of psychology.

By comparison, the human skeleton at the core of every human body is essentially the same in all of us. It is impossible to identify individuals by looking at their skeletons, although we know at a glance that the skeleton in our view is human. Could it be there is the same kind of universal structure at the base of the human psychological system? However different we are from one another on the surface, at a deep level we all share psychological fundamentals that identify us as human.

Level One: Personality

Sigmund Freud and his followers were interested in how different personality forms emerge from social interactions with parents and important others during the early years of life. Like philosophers David Hume and John Locke, Freud maintained that you enter life a blank sheet (*tabula rasa*). In the course of your childhood certain things happen between you and your parents and these happenings will cause you to become a particular kind of personality in adult life. Later we will discuss how neuroscience now confirms many of Freud's ideas of how personality is formed.[2]

Not all families are the same, and so, naturally, formative experiences will differ greatly. This means *at the level of personality* there will be considerable diversity and big differences among people in their way of being in the world. Individuals who have had similar experiences to me during their formative years will be 'pretty much like me' in worldview, attitudes and behaviour and those who had different experiences will not. They may, in fact, be spectacularly different from me.

Have you ever met someone and after a brief time thought, 'What a brilliant, interesting, excellent individual!' It is clear to you that they should be given the job or your friendship or whatever membership is on offer. In this scenario it is likely that you have been relating to someone whose personality layer is the same as yours. They view the world in a similar way and so you feel a 'click' of recognition and validation.

It is a simple human reality that we nearly always think that people who agree with us are 'brilliant', 'interesting' and 'excellent'.

Alternatively, have you ever found yourself wondering 'Who is this person? Do they inhabit some parallel universe?' The answer is YES. Without a doubt, this individual had very different formative experiences to you and so views things in a very different way.

Because we operate in the world through our personalities, successful interpersonal exchanges will depend on developing an ability to discern when we are in the same psychological place as the other person or on another attitudinal planet entirely. Once we know where we are, we can – with skilled and mindful awareness – relate with sensitivity and attuned listening that will lead to positive results.

The Centaur model describes five unique personality styles that are distinct from one another in their formative history and, therefore, in the way they operate in the world. Each type requires a markedly different approach if good contact and a positive outcome are to be achieved.

Level Two: An Essential Core

Carl Jung and those he influenced were less concerned with the personality self formed during the early years of childhood. They focused instead on a 'spiritual essence' at the core of human nature – called the SELF – that is present before any of the social learning that forms personality takes place.[3]

Jung's views are similar to those of philosophers like Socrates, Plato, Hegel and Kant. All shared a conviction that an ethical core of goodness underpins our psychology. Plato maintained that a sense of the 'True', the 'Good' and the 'Beautiful' forms the structural basis of our psychology in the same way as our skeletal system underpins our physical bodies.

These philosophical thinkers proposed that we can access and be guided by this inner resource through a process of committed self-awareness. If this ethical SELF deep inside forms part of our answer to the (metaphysical) question 'Who am I?', then we each have a life-long journey to discover and then to express this original (and ethical) nature in the way we live with others. Socrates famously stated, 'The unexamined life is not worth living.'

What would it be like if our definition of good leadership included not only commercial effectiveness in the outside world, but also a connection to ethical responsibility within?

As is the case with the Golden Rule ('Do unto others as you would have them do unto you'), all of the great religions and most philosophies share this contention that there is a principle of goodness within each of us that is meant to guide our life. Later we will discuss how these ideas are mirrored in exciting new thoughts within the domain of theoretical science.

It is at this fundamental, core level that the Golden Rule applies, calling on us to pay attention to this positive aspect within ourselves and to acknowledge it in others through respectful interaction. Every one of us has a right to be treated with respect. Respect is the most important thing of all in relating with other people at work or anywhere else.

I have explored this proposition with thousands of my students over the years, asking if the following statement felt true for them:

'Within the work context, if you treat me with respect, I will *give* you what you cannot *buy* with money or *coerce* through fear.'

The answer has been unanimously affirmative.

We are all deeply – even if unconsciously – aware of our intrinsic value, and so we long for and *require* respectful treatment. And from this same level of awareness we are inclined to treat others with respect. When at our best we *reciprocate* respect with respect. Another name for the Golden Rule is the 'Ethic of Reciprocity'.

Sadly, we do not always achieve this. Nevertheless, when we fail to live out this fundamental principle we are likely to experience a felt sense of misalignment and disappointment or even shame. At such moments Socrates would recommend that we 'examine our lives' and correct our behaviour.

Translated into a language for the workplace, the Golden Rule or Ethic of Reciprocity might read, 'Extend to others the respect that you would appreciate for yourself.'

It really is that simple, and yet it is very far from easy.

Because *at the level of personality, what is received and perceived as 'respect' differs radically from one personality type to another.* This is why well-intentioned individuals can make big mistakes in their interactions with others.

The Centaur model charts two levels of human psychology: a *core* nature, which is the same in all of us, and a *personality* level, where we can differ greatly from one another. Centaur further provides a strikingly practical lens for identifying personality types, along with clear guidance as to how to approach each type in a way that leads to a good outcome.

Two Levels: A Metaphor

Imagine that all human beings are born a vast garden of potential, bursting with every possible bloom and blossom and that these potentials are grounded in a rich soil of natural morality. Within this metaphorical garden all of the positive characteristics listed below in the definitions of each of the five Centaur personality types are potentials within every one of us.

When we are born into the world of others, our parents, and later the wider family and then our social and cultural context, indicate to us which of our possibilities are valued by them. In response, we reach inside and collect a bouquet of potentials that match what is wanted, present it to the world and say, 'Here I am – please love me'.

This is a simplified picture of how our personality is created, but it captures the essence of the process, which will be outlined in detail in Chapter Two. Most importantly, this image further suggests the vast potential that lies untapped within each of us.

Although your personality is often all you consciously *know of yourself*, it represents only a part of your true potential. The Centaur approach invites you to think more deeply about who you are and what you might become.

Five Personality Types

Five personality types are outlined and demonstrated in detail in Chapter Two. Briefly these are:

The **Magicals: (Wizards and Sprites)** are known for their creative thinking and imagination. These individuals have an ability to see things from a number of perspectives. They typically have very high principles and perfectionistic standards. Magicals can struggle with what they consider constraints within conventional processes at work and elsewhere. They may need help in dealing with organizational reality and in maintaining relaxed relationships with colleagues at work.

The **Romantics (Damsels and Poets)** are often valued for their easy and charming interpersonal manner that can enliven a team or bring a difficult client on board. When combined with a stronger aspect (like Hero especially) this personality thread provides an added asset of sensitivity to the latter's hard-edged problem-solving skills. However, when Romantic is the dominant aspect of personality, an individual may need support with motivation along with developmental interventions that will require them to build the stamina to finish projects and meet standards.

The **Superheroes (Supermen and Wonder Women)** are typically famous for their lateral and opportunistic thinking. These individuals are often a valuable asset to a team or organization, but they can be a challenge to manage. They are typically charismatic and inspiring, taking their teams into further reaches of success through unexpected and intuitive moves. Like the Magicals above, Superheroes struggle with conventional rules and guidelines. Moreover, they are inclined to really push boundaries or even jump right over them. In these cases, they need grounded colleagues (like Guardians and Heroes) to provide important limits for their exuberance.

The **Guardians (Earth Mothers and Good Fathers)** are invariably valued for their reliability and steadfast dedication to both their teams and the task at hand. These – along with the Heroes – are the backbone of good corporate business. Guardians think of others and they play by the rules, affording a very 'low maintenance' and 'high value' resource within the corporate community. At times their attendance to others and to the rules keeps them from promoting themselves into leadership positions for which they both technically and morally qualify. Then they need others to give them an encouraging push on their way up the ladder of leadership.

The **Heroes (Warriors and Huntresses)** are realistic, rational and law-abiding. They are valued for their clear thinking, direct approach and determination to 'get things done'. High ambition is a key feature of Heroes and fairness is a central value. They are dedicated to winning, but the win must be achieved 'fair and square'. In their striving to succeed, Heroes can lose track of the feelings of others and/or become overly rational and rigid in their thinking. Advice from a Guardian, who is good at connecting with the feelings of others, can help in the first instance and a Magical colleague, who 'thinks outside the box', with the second. The question is, will this strong and independent personality ask for help?

Of course nothing human is as tidy as five distinct boxes. Indeed, the human spirit recoils from being boxed in any case. I must admit that I have this same response to labels and discrete types that contain and limit how we see ourselves.

When considering the Centaur types, please don't think of boxes. Imagine instead five pots of paint, which contain the three primary colours of red, blue and yellow along with the absolutes of black and white. Then think of how many colours, shades and hues you can create from these five pots. The answer is literally 'all of them'. Many people are a mix of two or even three of the Centaur personality types and you can learn how to discern these different aspects within yourself and in others.

Moreover, beyond 'boxes' and even 'colours', Centaur invites you to embrace the notion of a whole level of untapped potential within. Your personality – whether a mix or singular type – represents only a limited and edited version of your true potential.

THE MOST IMPORTANT PRINCIPLE OF CENTAUR WORK IS: THERE IS MORE TO YOU THAN YOU THINK, AND IT IS POSITIVE.

Once you have this kind of awareness then dramatic change and growth are possible. Author Stephen Johnson uses the word 'character' to designate what I am calling 'personality'. The title of his seminal volume, *Characterological Transformation: The Hard Work Miracle*, aptly evokes the challenge of the personal development path. You can make exciting and 'transformational'

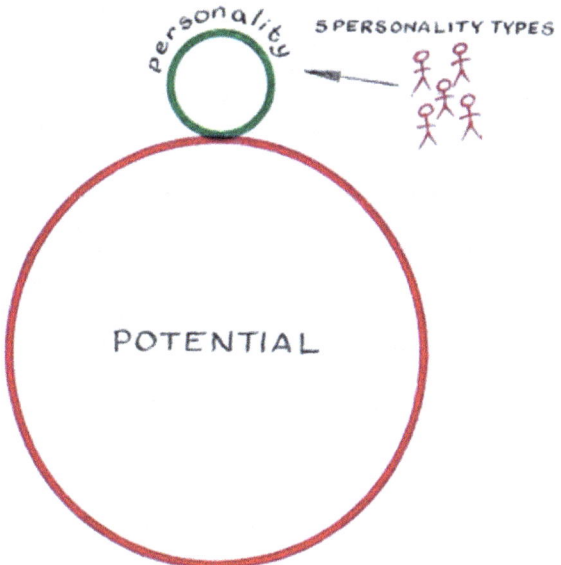

changes in your personality or character, says Johnson, *and it takes committed hard work.* The Centaur approach is a good map for this journey both in regard to developing yourself and in relating to others.

THE MOST PRACTICAL PRINCIPLE OF CENTAUR WORK IS: OTHERS CAN BE DIFFERENT FROM YOU (in personality) AND STILL VALID.

When you approach another personality, you enter a separate psychological space, which may be similar to your own type or vastly different. *We are all the same* in our requirement to be treated with respect and we all have the same positive response to being met and regarded in this way. However, *we differ greatly* in what we each require from another person in order to feel that we are respected.

Each personality type has a specific definition of 'respect' and learning who requires what in order to feel valued and respected is a key offering of the Centaur approach.

The case study below highlights this dilemma, showing how a well-intentioned individual does very well with a colleague of his own type but unknowingly blunders in increasingly marked and spectacular modes with others who need something different from him as a leader if they are to feel respected and thence be motivated, enthused and inspired.

This example below provides an illustration of the difficulties of dealing with others effectively. Centaur offers a practical and effective solution, which is outlined in specific detail in Chapter Two.

A Case Study

Peter is a Hero personality type. Hero personalities easily identify with gender designations of 'Warrior' and 'Huntress'. The orientating worldview of the Hero (Warrior/Huntress) is based on the excitement of challenge and the thrill of winning. Heroes value independence and responsibility and they do not like asking others for help.

As will be explained in due course, the Hero is a well-developed personality form but the following case study demonstrates what happens when a psychologically robust person operates in the frame of mind 'Everybody is pretty much like me' in the daily context of a corporate setting.

The Situation

Peter comes in on a Monday morning to a challenge. A project he is in charge of has gone awry. A complex and urgent response is necessary: clients need to be contacted and reassured. Internal resources must be mobilized and his team of project managers (PMs) needs to reprioritize their day to meet the emergency and maintain the company's good reputation for delivery.

The Hero personality loves a challenge and Peter springs energetically and optimistically into action. He calls in each of his project managers in turn and initiates his response to the emergency.

Peter greets each PM with a quick appraisal of the situation. No small talk. Even in relaxed times Peter dislikes chitchat on the job. He keeps his social and private life separate from work. In a crisis this 'no time wasting' attitude is exaggerated. Heroes are logical and rational, and Peter quickly devises an overall plan of action. He delegates a sizeable part of the plan to each of his PMs, saying, 'Here are your resources; let me know if you need anything more. If I don't hear from you, I will see you at the Wednesday meeting when I will expect to have this issue under control. Good luck!'

In the above scenario, Peter treats his project managers in precisely the way he would want to be managed in such a situation.

As discussed above, the Centaur model presents five personality types each with an unconscious worldview that affects how they think and act. Let us use this scenario to explore these differing personality types and highlight how the Centaur lens can lead to more effective and inspirational leadership.

PM 1: Joan is the same personality type as Peter. She is a Hero Huntress and holds the same unconscious worldview which values independence, challenge and responsibility. The unconscious worldview of the Hero type can be summarised as:

- *I am an independent and capable person.*
- *Others should be treated fairly.*
- *The world is an adventure.*

Joan is energised by the crisis and feels seen and valued when her manager wants her to take responsibility for a sizeable aspect of the solution. Joan is glad that Peter gets straight to the point, avoiding time-wasting conversations about their respective weekends. She is inspired by Peter's confidence in her and is determined that she will not have to ask for help in completing her assigned part of the task.

Monday has started well for Joan and it is likely that she will deliver a quality piece of work at the meeting on Wednesday.

There is an optimal way to manage a Hero personality style and – because he and Joan share the same worldview – Peter has hit it exactly right. Joan will operate to her full potential. She will take responsibility and execute her remit with energy and good will. The task is likely to succeed and the organization will be well served.

PM 2: In terms of personality strength, the Guardian is every bit as realistic and committed to the task as the Hero. Guardians (the 'Good Father' and the 'Earth Mother') want to get things done every bit as much as the Hero. However, of equal importance to them is the value of courtesy and cordial contact between people. When this sense of interpersonal regard is missing Guardians may become disaffected and offended. The unconscious worldview of the Guardian can be summarized as:

- *I am a good person.*

- *Others deserve courtesy.*

- *The world should be a good place for people.*

With these attitudes at the back of his mind, Guardian George has a rather different reaction to Peter's management style. He is offended by the lack of basic politeness when greeted on a Monday morning – crisis or no crisis. After all, how long does it take to say, 'Good morning, how was your weekend?'

George dislikes the way Peter sees people as 'mechanistic parts in his success machine'. He agrees with Peter that the task is important and he will take his allocated responsibilities seriously. George will show up on Wednesday with a good offering. However, he will fulfil these responsibilities grudgingly and stoically because it is the right thing to do and not because he is motivated by his leader.

The week has not started well for George. He leaves Peter's office in a mood of resentment and his respect for Peter as a leader – already low due to previous similar encounters – is further eroded.

There is an optimal way to manage a Guardian personality style. At their best Guardians are splendid colleagues. They are warm-hearted and hard-working with huge energetic resources. They typically give well beyond what is expected of them. Peter's Hero approach is off the mark with Guardian George. A valuable and trustworthy human resource is disaffected as a result. George will do his duty but he will not be forthcoming with his good will and his extra 10 per cent of effort.

PM 3: Patrick is bold, talented and unpredictable. The most important thing for Patrick at work is personal impact and brand. He has the charismatic and exciting presence of the Centaur type called Superhero. The motivation of the Superhero 'Wonder Woman' and 'Superman' has less to do with the success of the task than with personal charisma and power.

Superheroes do not like being told what to do, so Patrick finds Peter's briefing style irritating and diminishing. Furthermore, the Superhero's thinking style is lateral and opportunistic, so Patrick feels cramped by Peter's logical approach. He often complains that Peter never seems to understand what he has to offer. Events in the formative years of the Superhero produce an unconscious worldview that can be summarized as:

- *I am/should be on top.*
- *Others are not as good as me.*
- *The world is my oyster.*

Because Patrick feels irritated and unappreciated, he is unlikely to fully engage with the project and may do an off-target or poor job. Any failures will typically be made the responsibility of others. Patrick leaves Peter's office uncommitted, out of sorts and on his way to do whatever will make him feel important and look good in the eyes of others, especially those in power.

There is an optimal way to manage a Superhero personality style that will reassure their self-esteem and harness their exuberance in service of the task.

Superheroes, compared to Guardians and Heroes, are high-maintenance. However, when handled well they are a resource of ingenuity and energy within an organization. They are frequently brilliant with clients and often inspire their own teams to remarkable success.

For a Superhero, Peter's Hero approach is a disaster. As a result, an energetic and lateral mind is set against the success of the task because a difference in worldview has not been taken into account. Patrick does not feel respected by Peter and no good can come from this.

PM 4: Julie is a classic example of a fourth Centaur type. The Romantic ('Poet' and 'Damsel') is not interested in power like the Superhero. They thrive on the social and relational aspects of work and are motivated by contact with others rather than success of the task or being given positions of authority. Romantics relate to others through charm and social grace rather than charisma or logic.

The Romantics value interpersonal connection like the Guardians, but unlike the Guardians, the success of the task is not at the top of their agenda. Most important for Romantics is the social exchange between people and the fun of interpersonal relationships. The Romantic can be a real asset to the team, forging valuable relationships with clients and charming difficult situations into successful outcomes. They are often brilliant at presentations where grace and ease with people are important.

Although talented in the important ways described above, Romantics are not robust. Whereas the Guardians identify with giving to other people, Romantics unconsciously look to others to meet their needs and fuel their sometimes flagging energetic resources. This can leave colleagues feeling drained as a result. Unfortunate events early on in the formative years of a Romantic lead to a worldview that can be summarized as:

- *I am in need.*
- *Others in charge should be looking after me.*
- *The world owes me a living.*

With this psychological orientation, Julie has a terrible reaction to Peter's leadership style. Romantic Julie is not driven by success of the task like Hero Joan. She feels overwhelmed by the responsibility that Peter gives her and abandoned by his assumption that she will share his attitude of independence and responsibility.

As a Romantic, Julie lacks the constitutional energetic resources of the previous three personality styles. When Peter hands her the entire responsibility for her part of the task, Julie feels lost. She will very likely find diversions that will take her away from her discomfort and then make excuses for her failure to deliver. Over time, the pressure of such situations may lead her to take time off work with stress-related conditions.

There is an optimal way to manage Romantics that brings out their best qualities and helps develop them toward a mature work ethic. In the chapter on Practical Application, specific suggestions as to how to encourage Romantics to become more resilient and task focused are outlined.

Peter thought he was treating Julie with respect. Sadly, his Hero approach led to demotivation and distress, which eclipse Julie's qualities of charm and interpersonal ease that are the valuable contribution of this personality type to the spirit of a team and relationships with clients.

PM 5: The Magical personality form is perhaps the most delicate of the five Centaur types. However, what the 'Wizard' and 'Sprite' bring to the team can be what makes the biggest difference to the product or the strategy and therefore to the survival of an organization.

The Magicals specialize in creative and innovative thinking and frequently come up with wonderfully different perspectives and solutions. Like the Romantic or the Superhero, they need focused and mindful management if they are to give their gifts to the situation. Frightening experiences in the very early life of the Magical have led to an unconscious worldview that can be summarized as:

- *I am fragile.*
- *Others can be hostile.*
- *The world is dangerous.*

Magical Sam is shocked and strained by Peter's forthright challenge to take on this high-pressure assignment. What was a pleasure for Joan and a satisfying duty for George is a harrowing pressure for Sam.

Unlike the Romantic, the Magical Wizard/Sprite will not avoid the task. They tend to over-commit, becoming perfectionist and obsessing unnecessarily over details. The task may be well done but timelines will suffer and Sam is likely to become stressed and in due course dysfunctional because of too much pressure, albeit much of his own making.

There is an optimal way to manage a Magical that provides a sense of safety and protection, within which they can give their frequently remarkable contribution.

Hero Peter would feel offended at the thought of being protected by his manager. Assuming 'everybody is like me' it does not occur to him to provide the context Magical Sam needs to give his brilliant best. Peter meant well, but his Hero approach puts this valuable individual under undue strain. Sam does not feel respected, he feels threatened and trapped.

The Centaur model offers a theoretical framework that deepens insight and practical skills that foster emotional attunement. These provide informed perceptions of colleagues, clients and also members of the board. A deepened understanding of who we are and the nature of other people is the key to good outcomes in all of these relationships.

What next?

In Chapter One – *An Invitation to be Psychological* – a description of the formation of personality is explained through the lenses of classical psychology along with compelling notions from both neuroscience and the mathematical principles of Complexity Theory.

In Chapter Two – *Practical Application* – the developmental crucible that forms each personality type is described, along with how they appear in the workplace in terms of their gifts and their developmental issues. This is followed by an outline of the effective approach to each of the five types, which is summarized under the heading 'Mindful Management' at the end of each of the five sections on the personality types.

In Chapter Three – *Reflections* – we return to the questions posed in the Introductions – 'Who am I?' and 'How should I live with others?' Some final frameworks, inspirational ideas and heartening examples will be reviewed.

Notes

1. The Golden Rule (Ethic of Reciprocity): Internet Reference
2. Gay, P. (1988) *Freud: A Life for Our Time*. London: J.M. Dent & Sons Ltd.
3. Storr, A. (1998) *The Essential Jung*. London: Fontana Press

CHAPTER ONE:
An Invitation to Be Psychological

FREUD AND NEUROSCIENCE
An Unconscious Worldview Runs Your Life

'Who knows what frescoes are painted on the back wall of our minds?'

Isadora Duncan

Around the beginning of the twentieth century Sigmund Freud radically changed how we human beings view ourselves. Whilst some of his groundbreaking theories have been superseded, two remain central to how all of us think about ourselves today. These are: that we have an unconscious as well as a conscious mind and that during the first five years of our lives we establish a template of attitudes – a worldview – that influences us for the rest of our lives.[1]

Until Freud, the tendency had been to believe that however chaotic and confusing events were round about us, at least we knew what was going on in our own minds. This certainty faded away in the light of Freud's doctrine of the 'unconscious mind', where some of the most important causes of our mental lives lie totally hidden from us.

Freud maintained that we are influenced in everyday life by archaic attitudes and impulses of which we are quite unaware. We believe we live our lives on a rational basis but unconscious patterns lay invisible hands on the steering wheel of all of us.

Where do these powerful and primitive attitudes originate? Freud established the crucial importance of experiences in early childhood on the development of our adult way-of-being-in-the-world, our personality. He named the first five years of a child's life the 'formative years'. During this critical time, through ongoing interaction with parents and family, a child gathers a deeply inscribed 'worldview' represented by the completion of these three sentence stems:

- *I am…*
- *Others are…*
- *The world is…*

The learning that creates our worldview is not thought about cognitively in the way we typically 'think' in adult life. It is based on what we experience bodily and emotionally. Much of this experience occurs before we are able to think in the way we typically understand thinking.

Early experiences – absorbed through the interpersonal atmosphere engendered by caregivers – are encoded deep within our minds and bodies in powerful archaic memories. These fundamental memories are the fabric of our personality. They create a tacit understanding of self, others and the world. This foundational worldview lies beyond the edge of consciousness even in adult life. In this way a worldview established in our earliest years becomes an unconscious template of being that shapes our lives, influencing what we feel about ourselves, how we respond to others and the way we look at the world.

Neurobiologist Daniel Siegel defines memory as 'An experience in the past that shapes us in the present and affects how we will act and think and behave in the future.' He cautions that memory is more than 'what comes to mind when we try to recall something'. Memory, he says, does not have to be conscious nor in awareness nor known about. Memory includes what we can recall but – as Freud suggested – it is much bigger than that.[2]

Memory

Both Freud and modern neuroscientists like Daniel Siegel, Allan Schore and Bessel van der Kolk maintain that our sense of who we are is literally composed of memories. The classic view of the human mind as a blank sheet (*tabula rasa*) on which concrete experiences etch an identity is central to this view.

Through the lens of neuroscience, we can picture a newborn human brain as a vast starry firmament full of millions and millions of points of cellular light. These 'neuronal stars' are brain cells that are alive and blazing and waiting for outside events to cause them to fire and connect with one another, forming patterns of experiences – memories – that chart joyous incidents and/or telling ordeals as a new life encounters the world of other people.

We know that this vast number of neurons multiplies up until the age of twenty-four months when unused cells begin to be naturally pruned away. It is crucial for the survival of brain cells and hence mental capacity that babies are regularly stimulated so that these neurons link up with one another and so avoid pruning. If neurons are not wired into patterns by interactive experience they will be washed away in a cleansing biochemical wash that occurs around age two.[3]

This neurobiological fact has relevance to ideas about good parenting. When a human baby is not socially engaged, loved and stimulated, potential is lost and vitality is compromised. Neurologist Allan Schore proclaims, 'Cells that fire together wire together and survive together.'[3]

The Formation of a Worldview

This firing up of patterns in the brain is the way that personality and worldview form. The difference between joyful, life-affirming experiences and difficult, disappointing events plays a significant part in determining whether the orientating attitudes of an individual will be positive or negative, optimistic or pessimistic and if energetic responsiveness will be resilient or compromised.

Our worldview is built on memories. Schore suggests that a mother (or caregiver) literally 'sculpts' the shape of her baby's brain. Within this same artistic range of metaphor we can say that repeated experiences in childhood paint an archaic fresco onto the back wall of our minds and that these images and narratives represent our individual sense of truth and reality based on lived experience.

We have all seen pictures in astronomy books or looked through a telescope to see the firmament of a night sky alight with stars. In the books, these stars are connected by lines that reveal the constellations that articulate the heavens and give shape to that starry vastness, making it readable to us in images of heroes and their stories.

Neurologists invite us to picture an inner firmament, full of neuronal stars, which are articulated by our own defining patterns of images and stories – the neural pathways that our young brains wire up in our quest to make sense of the world. These pathways and orientations constitute the physical dimension of a worldview that can last a lifetime.

This metaphor is congruent with the terminology of psychologists who say that a child 'constellates' a set of attitudes in response to experiences with important others in their formative years. Such attitudes – built upon memories – underpin enduring habits of perceiving, thinking and acting that shape our lives. Our memories are quite literally the basis of our way of being in the world.

The Structure of the Brain

Memory is located in the emotional centre of the brain, which is called the limbic system. The limbic system is one of three distinct parts of the human brain, each of which is profoundly different from the others. All have an important part to play in understanding ourselves and others.

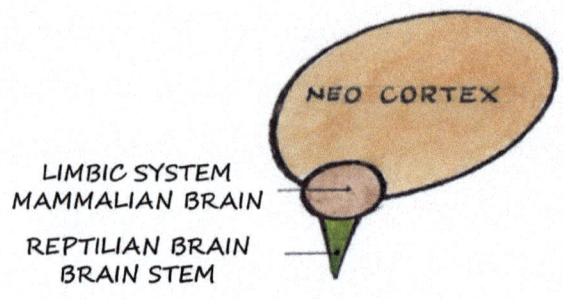

The deepest and most primitive part of your brain is called the 'brain stem'. Put your hand on the back of your neck and move your head from side to side – that is roughly the location of your brain stem. The brain stem is home to our most basic functions: heart rate, arousal patterns, blood pressure, for example. This deeply unconscious and primary aspect of your brain is colloquially called the 'reptilian brain' because we share this kind of brain function with our reptilian cousins.

Now move your hand up to the curved-out part of your skull and focus on a spot in line with your hand but deep inside your head. This is the location of the second part of your triune, or three-part, brain. At the top of the brain stem and in the centre of the skull flowers the 'limbic system', which is often referred to as our 'mammalian brain'. This mammalian brain houses very different functions from the brain stem.

The limbic system is called the 'seat of emotions' and it is the source of our relationships with others. Reptiles have neither emotions nor relationships. For example, when reptile babies are born they typically flee from their parents, arguably because reptiles have such bad eyesight that parents are likely to mistake their young for prey and eat them. By classic Darwinian rule, reptile babies run as soon as they are born in order to survive.

Mammalian babies do the opposite. They turn toward their mothers, and if a relational bond of nurture, protection and connection is not made, they will perish. This need for relationship is critical for all of us warm-blooded mammalian creatures. We need others in order to first survive and then later to thrive in life. In fact, this need for others is inscribed organically in the developmental sequence of our brains. Researcher Dan Siegel maintains that the mammalian brain cannot successfully complete its maturation without adequate interaction with another brain.[2] Studies of survival data from concentration camps of World War Two consolidate these ideas, charting that those who survived the death camps tended to be individuals who made nurturing and supportive relationships with others. Such poignant findings are underlined in the implacable statement, 'The unit of human survival is two, never one.'

Indeed, survival and safety are the first and primary concern of a newborn human being. And so it is no surprise that the most basic level of the limbic system is the fear circuitry, which centres on a little almond-shaped 'alarm bell' called the 'amygdala' that signals danger through the release of powerful biochemicals and hormones.

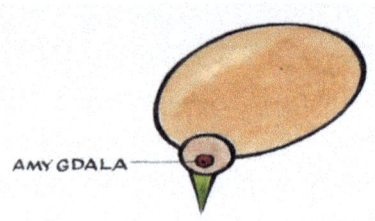

When the amygdala is triggered over-much in babyhood, it has a negative effect on the emerging worldview of a child. Too much experience of fear shapes a worldview based on fright and it will be lacking in natural confidence. Later we will observe how it also significantly affects the development of the physical body.

As we will discuss shortly, the first right or need of the formative years is the right to *exist*, which is confirmed to a newborn through a warm welcome that assures safety and security.

In addition to being the seat of our emotions, the limbic system is also the location of memories, which form the basis of our primary and often unconscious orientations toward life. Repeated memories from early life lay down those deeply encoded attitudes toward self, others and the world that shape how we live. No matter how much we would like to think that we do what we do based on our reason and logic, neuroscience confirms that what actually runs our daily lives are these fundamental attitudes inscribed in resonant emotional layers of memory at the very back of our minds.

Arching over the limbic system is a third part of the brain – called the new or 'neo' cortex – which is found in higher primates and human beings.

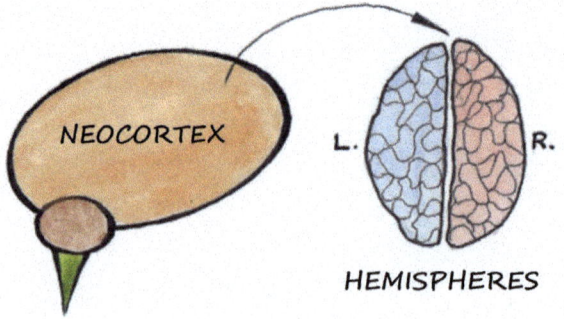

The neocortex is composed of the two cerebral hemispheres and represents a dramatic addition to functioning in human and other primate brains.

Although the neocortex does occur in higher primates, in human beings it is so huge and its unique capacities are so spectacularly delineated that in this brief introduction it might rightly be named the 'human brain'.

All mammals have feelings and emotions but only human beings have the ability featured in the neocortex to 'think about' feelings and emotions and to decide whether to express them and in what manner. Its two cerebral hemispheres are the largest and most obvious features of this 'human' brain. The surface grey matter of these hemispheres is made up of densely packed nerve fibres tightly folded into an outer lid covering the subcortical structures which include the limbic system. The word 'cortex' comes from the Latin word for the bark of a tree. The neocortex is a thick bark covering older (subcortical) parts of the brain.

Shortly we will discuss how the left and the right hemisphere differ dramatically from one another in both structure and function. For now, we return to the limbic system and the all-important function of memory in the formation of our way-of-being-in-the-world that is our personality.

The Nature of Memory

Memory is not logical. Our memories are not formed by anything remotely like reasoning. Memory is an *associational* process wherein things that happen at the same time become linked together often in a random and illogical manner. In this way, disparate events such as perceptions, emotions and bodily sensations wire up together in a network that forms a particular and distinct memory. This associational principle provides important insight into what memory is and how it impinges on our daily lives.

By way of an example, last spring I was sitting with my friend Carol on the patio adjacent to my garden. While the temperature was warm the day was grey and threatening to be rainy. Carol and I were reflecting on how happy we were with the unfolding of a project we had hatched between us. There was much laughter and a gentle lightness of mood.

We decided to walk down my long and narrow garden, visiting my extensive collection of camellias and magnolias and the promise of my roses. We reached the end of the garden where a hugely blooming red rhododendron held sway. At the sight of the rhododendron I suddenly felt my mood shift and positively soar in utter delight. I turned to Carol to share this only to see her close to tears, her face shadowed and troubled. At the moment of my upward swing of emotion, she had dropped into an inner pit of misery.

We were so struck by this contrast that we determined to explore what had happened to each of us, most especially to her. Clearly the red rhododendron had been the 'trigger' for both of us and so, in real Freudian fashion, we 'free associated' to rhododendrons. We each opened our imagination to any thought or image that came to mind when we focused on this big red bush.

Both of us came quickly to a strong memory that matched our change in mood. I remembered being on a romantic holiday in Scotland with a much-loved new partner some years ago. Our hotel had been located at the base of what seemed a miles-long corridor of fully blooming rhododendrons blasting red and pink against a grey Scottish sky, which only enhanced their vibrant colour. My beloved was not much given to expressing tender feelings. However, on a walk among these flowers he told me he loved me for the first time. It was that fantastic memory that ignited in me when I saw my big red 'rhodi' against the grey sky that day with Carol. I was transported into feelings of optimistic delight and happiness.

Carol's memory of rhododendrons was very different. A child of army-based, expatriate parents, she had spent her first six years in the far east where the weather was hot and sunshine seemed ever present. The family's lifestyle was affluent, with servants and existed within a social whirl. Carol was warmly cared for by a native nanny and had the kind of lovely, focused time with her parents that such a lifestyle allows. When Carol was six her father was relocated to Manchester where he took up a promising post at the university. It was a good career move. However, the family's living style changed dramatically. In Manchester there were no servants to help when a second baby arrived in the spring, bringing on a severe case of post-natal depression for her mother. In order to ease the pressure at home and to give Carol 'children to play with', she was sent away every weekend to stay with another family down the road. Not surprisingly, she was desperately unhappy, feeling banished from home and (as children do) somehow responsible for what was wrong. The pavements of the neighbourhood she lived in were edged by huge rhododendron bushes, which flanked and coloured her weekly walk to a miserable and lonely weekend. What came into Carol's consciousness on seeing my red rhododendron was the memory of a cold, rainy Manchester spring where she felt lonely and desolate.

This story demonstrates how things that happen at one simultaneous time become linked to each other in an unconscious 'cluster'. These clusters are composed of emotions, perceptions, bodily actions and sensations, which are tied together through association. The stimulation of any single aspect of the cluster can trigger the entire network of feelings and sensations into awareness.

This can have a powerful effect on a present moment as was the case with Carol and me. The triggering aspect of 'rhododendrons' surfaced dramatically different changes of mood within each of us as we were overtaken by a 'blast from the past'. Because of our training and the gift of time, we were able to identify the source of our emotions but this is not always the case. A more serious example of this process in a professional context is illustrated in the story below.

'What has come over me?'

Nancy is a bright and promising professional woman in her mid-twenties. She grew up in a well-to-do middle-class family with a loving mother and a brilliant but perfectionist father whom she very much admired. As Nancy progressed through school her father took great interest in her academic success. He expressed his love for her through what was arguably an over-rigorous attention to her homework along with expectations for highest grades and top-of-the-class performance. Nancy reported that he had an 'eagle eye' for detail and what he considered careless mistakes were not tolerated. His often stated philosophy was 'anything worth doing is worth doing 100 per cent'.

Through experience of her father's perfectionism in her formative years, Nancy developed an inner picture of a powerful and admired male figure based on a *perception* of her father's strict and perfectionistic look, an *emotion* of trepidation and anxiety of being unable to meet his standards, a *bodily action* to withdraw and hide from his scrutiny and also *bodily sensations* of tension in her shoulders and nausea in her stomach. These last physical events happened because Nancy's body was reacting to alarm signals from her amygdala – that little almond-shaped panic button at the core of the limbic system which triggered cascades of stress biochemicals and hormones into her system causing digestive upset and muscular tension. Over time this kind of physiological response can become part of the implicit cluster of associated happenings and these bodily events can spontaneously ignite years later when a present-day perception activates the unconscious memory cluster.

This bodily aspect of memory is called 'priming', where the nervous system automatically gets ready to respond in a certain kind of way. The triggering event is often 'subliminal' – that is out of awareness – causing old feelings, perceptions and bodily sensations to occur without warning or understanding. Such a process is illustrated below in Nancy's story.

Some years after leaving home Nancy – now an established professional – was asked to present her prized project to the chairman of her company. She was baffled to find herself alarmingly tense and on edge 'for no apparent reason'. She found herself unable to concentrate when organizing her thoughts. Her sleep was disturbed and her confidence suffered.

Nancy's attitudinal past was 'laying invisible hands' on her current life. She was caught up in an old – out of consciousness – attitude toward male authority. A cluster of mental, emotional and physical events in her childhood had 'fired and wired' together in reaction to her admired and perfectionistic father, constellating an unconscious template for responding to a male authority within a performance context.

This spontaneous triggering of an unconscious cluster of memories may be happening to any one of us when we say to ourselves or one another, 'What has come over me/you?' Because the process is unconscious, we have no answers.

Within each of us our unconscious brims with memory clusters that can spring to life – for better as well as for worse – when events in the present stimulate any one of the associated aspects within a cluster. In this way, our past is always with us, affecting how we see and experience current events. Dan Siegel confidently proclaims, 'There is no such thing as immaculate perception.' We see everything through the lens of our unconscious worldview, which is woven of memories and located deep within the limbic system in our brains.[2]

The sound of people laughing around a kitchen table may evoke in one person a loving childhood memory complete with vivid images and sweet and powerful feelings of safety and acceptance, while another hears the same laughter and experiences a wave of humiliation and shame called up out of a less happy resource of implicit memory.

In this same regard, the look on the face of a boss or an important client can evoke confidence-boosting memories of a supportive grandparent or alternatively a painful unconscious cluster 'wired in' by the experience of a harsh teacher at school. Negative 'blasts from the past' lead to misperception, misunderstanding and missed opportunities. Protagonists are hijacked by a 'forgotten' experience and transported emotionally back to another time. 'What has come over me?' they may well ask.

The 'examined' life – recommended by Socrates – requires us to stay with that question 'What has come over me?' in order to find the root of the issue and then take the route of curiosity and awareness that leads to change and development.

The Centaur model can be a helpful guide in this process. It is important that we each become interested in what happens within our emotional process. *When we identify undermining memory clusters and move them from our unconscious into consciousness we release locked and frozen potential within us and in this way we can make our lives larger.*

Returning to our story, Nancy asks herself 'What has come over me?' as she experiences these troubling feelings when approaching her meeting with the Chairman who is keen to review her project. She *reasons* with herself, saying that she is both fluent with her material and convinced that it will be good for the company. She tries to reassure herself, reviewing the fact that she knows the Chairman personally and both respects his ethical stance and admires his concise commitment to excellence. She sees this clearly exhibited in *his intense and searching look when asking questions.*

Unknown to her, Nancy's perception of this look – so like that of her 'eagle-eyed' father – triggers into awareness the entire cluster of implicit memory connected with her perfectionist father. Without knowing why, she feels anxious and timid and very tense.

Logic and reason are surprisingly unhelpful when dealing with the emotional content of implicit memory. Later I will describe how rational processes are located in a different part of the brain from these triggered emotions, which are so stubbornly impervious to reason.

Nancy is helpless when this old emotional cluster is fired into life. She is gripped by an unconscious pattern that undermines her expression of her true potential. In order to free herself from this limiting grip, Nancy must access the capacity of another kind of memory that provides perspective, making the management of these unconsciously triggered events possible.

Two Kinds of Memory

i) Implicit Memory

In the brain there are two layers of memory: implicit memory, which is not in awareness; and explicit memory, which provides perspective through consciousness. Each of these can be associated with a key structure within the limbic system: the 'amygdala' and the 'hippocampus' respectively.

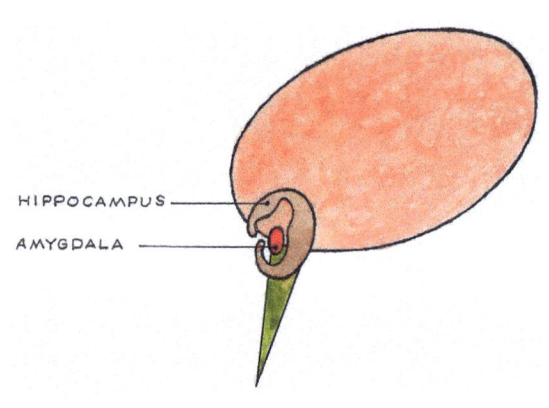

As described earlier the amygdala is active from the very start of life and is solely concerned with safety and security. The hippocampus comes 'online' around the age of two and has a more sophisticated remit.

As we have seen, implicit memory is the oldest kind of memory. This is indicated by its unconscious potency in Nancy's story. In fact, recent studies indicate that patterns of implicit memory are firing up in a baby's brain even before birth – within the third trimester in the womb. Daniel Siegel's charming yet rigorous experiment, which involved him singing particular songs to his unborn baby, evokes this research. Once born his infant daughter showed marked and measurable responses to the songs sung to her while she was in the womb; thus indicating that she had a memory of those particular tunes from before her birth.[2]

All experiences during the first year of life register at this deepest implicit level. These early experiences of babyhood have a profound and abiding effect on how we interact with other people throughout the rest of our lives. John Bowlby, a near contemporary of Freud, established through rigorous empirical research that our most basic way of connecting to others (he called it our 'attachment style') is fully in place *by the age of eleven months.*[4]

In the first year of life implicit memory registers deeply within our neural networks without any mitigating filter. In this way, a basic worldview about safety and trust is constellated early on which represents 'the truth as I have lived it'. It is important to flag here that what is 'assumed' to be happening by the baby may not be the 'actuality' of what really occurred. What forms the worldview is what the child 'makes of' what is happening as the impact of external events imprint upon the blank sheet of an innocent mind. This notion of 'assumed reality' will be more fully explored in the next chapter.

Throughout our lives we always lay things down first in this implicit form of memory, linking emotions, perception and bodily feelings together in clusters. In due course we generalize these experiences into a wider picture of how we see the world. However, for the first two years of life, *this is the only form of memory*, which is why babyhood and early toddler days are so powerful and influential in our development. There is no filter or framework, no perspective on experience. The non-rational, implicit patterns formed in the world of the baby and toddler are profound and they shape our perceptions and emotionally influence us throughout our lives without our knowing.

Referring back to our introductory case study, the debilitating anxiety of Magical Wizard Sam and the lack of energetic resilience of our Romantic Damsel Julie can be understood within this context of less than optimal 'babyhood wiring'. The specifics of these histories will be described in detail in the next chapter.

Imagine how helpful it might be to know at a glance when others have such unconscious inner predicaments and, further, how to provide a context that supports a good outcome between you and the person before you. These connections will be further explored in Chapter Two where the five personality types will be outlined in detail along with practical frameworks for creating respectful and effective relationships with each of them.

Moreover, further discussion will reveal that these same early life experiences paradoxically give Magical Sam and Romantic Julie unique gifts in adult life, which the attuned manager, leader or colleague can access through the mindful management techniques cited at the end of each personality section in Chapter Two.

Through the skill of 'soma reading' – literally tuning into a person's psychological make-up by observing patterns of bodily tension – Centaur alerts managers and leaders to such sensitivities and further provides guidance for appropriate interactions.

Centaur students report that this life-long gift of learned intuition is a conscious skill which they find themselves revisiting and benefitting from in all aspects of their lives.

ii) Explicit Memory

At around eighteen to twenty-four months of age a second crucial structure in the limbic system matures and activates. The 'hippocampus' is a seahorse-shaped area that lies adjacent to the amygdala deep in the limbic system. The hippocampus brings online a second kind of memory, which organizes and shapes implicit memories into more manageable experiences. This second kind of memory is called 'explicit' memory.

The hippocampus enables the building of this second layer of memory through establishing a sense of 'this is now' and 'that was then'. Adrift within a sea of implicit memory, an infant floats in an 'eternal now'. There is no perspective, no past or future. Each experience is total and forever. As maturation unfolds within a good babyhood, positive responses from the mother figure accumulate and are organized by the hippocampus into 'explicit' memories that *locate experiences in time*. In due course these anchored memories become *expectations* and the baby begins to have some purchase on the eternally flitting nature of experience. Ideally a core sense of stability takes shape so that if things are less than good on occasion, the baby is no longer overwhelmed by a bad 'now' because the hippocampus opens up the confident perspective that 'things are not so good at this moment, but they have been better and will get better again'.

In his extensive research into the development of resilience and confidence in babies and toddlers John Bowlby and his colleagues established how different kinds of parenting in babyhood produce a range of 'attachment' styles through which individuals relate in differing ways to disruptions in life.

In an ideal babyhood, there will have been many good experiences, and in due course the baby's hippocampus knits together a confident storyline resulting in what Bowlby called a 'secure' style of attachment. In this case, when an upset occurs, simple reassurance from a parent puts the 'secure' child back on track and all is well. However, if care and nurture have been patchy and unpredictable or chronically absent, the child develops either of two 'insecure attachment styles', discussed below, both of which will be chronicled into a narrative by the hippocampus.[4]

A child with an 'insecure/anxious' attachment style will not come to a state of repair easily. They will be seen clinging on to the parent figure for comfort and support yet apparently unable to settle. In a second insecure style – called 'insecure/dismissive' – the opposite is the case. The child appears to have given up hope of being helped by a parent and does not look to them for support and does not respond when help is offered. The really good news is that attachment research shows that through focus and effort individuals can heal these early wounds and establish – through an examined life – an 'earned secure' style of attachment.

With the growth of the hippocampus an awareness of the passage of time and therefore perspective becomes possible. A sense of order and a rudimentary sense of 'self' begins to take shape. The primitive fear circuitry centred on the alarm bell of the amygdala is contained and modulated as more advanced brain structures link deep limbic aspects to the more highly organized thinking capacities of the neocortex. A baby is hostage to a present and eternal moment, the child of two is developing the capacity to anticipate a change, hopefully for the better.

In this way happenings become more tolerable and differentiated and eventually 'good enough' experiences consolidate into a basis for a healthy worldview. In due course the developing child can begin to 'self soothe' rather being totally reliant on others. The mighty little amygdala is calmed and tamed. Its tendency to fright is put into perspective and mitigated by the organizing perspective provided by the hippocampus and other higher structures in the right hemisphere of the neocortex.

This capacity to move beyond the amygdala and primitive reactiveness is both physical and mental. We sense such a possibility and seek to build this capacity in our toddlers when we say 'use your words', encouraging them to express themselves more verbally and cognitively when they are in the midst of a surge of emotion and demand.

With the development of the hippocampus, *implicit* events become *explicitly* known and as a result they can be processed in a more organized manner. For example, when a child is very sad or angry, we hold them in our arms and in our gaze. We name the feeling, saying, 'Darling, you are so sad that the hamster died.' Or, 'You are really angry that Jonny broke your soldier.' When we name the feeling, the child gains awareness that they are *feeling* 'angry' or 'sad' rather than *being* 'anger' or 'sadness'. Through the naming and placing of experiences parents help children build a sense of self and so they become more self-aware and operate in the world with more consciousness.

As the hippocampus matures it begins to integrate the different jigsaw pieces of implicit memory into an organized pattern. Experiences are woven into a fabric of memories and expectations, building an integrated picture which is the basis of a growing worldview of *who* I am, *how* others are and *what* the world is like. The establishment of a robust hippocampus is an important part of psychological maturation.

When implicit data is processed through the hippocampus it is placed in a *frame of reference* and it is also *placed in time*. When an explicit memory is recalled to mind it is not a sudden surprise as are the triggering of implicit clusters like those discussed in my and Carol's experiences with the rhododendrons or in Nancy's story. When explicit memory is called into awareness, we have a felt sense that *what I am presently experiencing is coming from the past*. A response to what is recalled can be managed with awareness and therefore appropriate action taken.

How Centaur Provides Strategies and Solutions for Thriving

The Centaur remit for personal development encourages individuals to examine those moments when we ask, 'What has come over me?' Through exploring and 'thinking through' these moments we can often bring into consciousness the culprit cluster and deal with it rationally.

Bringing unconscious memory into awareness via the hippocampus places the intruding cluster of perception, emotions and bodily sensations into perspective. Placing such events into a time frame means we are less likely to unconsciously 'project' them onto people in our current daily life. For example, Nancy's chairman was a target for the unconscious 'projection' of her intimidating father. This 'transference' of memories and representations from the past into the events of our present happens all the time, especially with figures of authority. When the past 'projects' into our present in this way, inappropriate and disruptive events can erupt and we say, 'What has come over me?' Or 'What is going on with you?'

Centaur's teaching helps us to see individuals and events in our present without the distorting lens of an unexamined past. With some awareness of how our psychology works we can come to see our boss, our friend, our spouse, our teacher more clearly because our view of them is less contaminated by our personal history.

When Nancy has done appropriate 'process work' on her anxiety with male authority figures, she will have an inner resource of 'consciousness' to help her if she begins to feel tense when approaching a big meeting with an important man.

Centaur helps her to examine her reactions and stay with the question, 'What has come over me?' Having done this, Nancy may reflect: 'I know in my past my dad was strict and that made me nervous when I had to do something that mattered, but this is now and that was *then*. Moreover, the Chairman *is not my dad*!' She may continue her reflection, 'My history does make moments with important men at work a little tough for me, but I can handle it and the more I handle it the easier it gets.'

In summary, from babyhood as the brain develops, implicit networks and clusters of sensations and feelings are woven together by the hippocampus into a storyline that underpins a worldview of who I am with others in a certain kind of world. As the emotional brain grows up into the neocortex, an inner narrative emerges that consolidates the learning of our life's journey, which will have an impact on how we go forward and form a future.

A Self-Fulfilling Prophecy

Psychologists refer to this impact of our unconscious worldview on the way we live our daily life as a 'self-fulfilling prophecy'. Briefly, the self-fulfilling prophecy goes like this:

1. How I think about life (my unconscious worldview) affects how I approach life (most especially other people).

2. How I approach life (other people) affects the way life (other people) responds to me.

3. Therefore, I create the world I (unconsciously) expect!

A teaching tale from a famous medieval mystic called Rumi gives shape to the principle of a 'self-fulfilling prophesy'. It goes like this:

> A venerable monk sits begging halfway between two cities. A traveller passes by and as he gives the monk some coins asks, 'What is the character of this city I am approaching?'
>
> The monk enquires, 'What was it like in the city you left behind?'
>
> 'Kindly and generous,' replied the traveller. 'I made good business and found contentment there.'
>
> 'The city ahead of you is much the same; you will be happy there,' said the monk.
>
> Shortly thereafter a second traveller comes along and asks the beggar monk the same question.
>
> 'What is this city I approach like in character?'
>
> Again the monk enquires, 'What was the character of the city you left behind?'
>
> 'Why, it was aloof and unfriendly,' said the second traveller, 'and I was unhappy there.'
>
> 'I fear the city you move towards is much the same,' said the monk.

The moral of the tale confirms the extent to which we create our future from the inner expectations established within us by our past experiences.

The story of a coaching client of mine – let's call her Nell – provides a current narrative that makes this same point. Here is what happened. It was obvious to the head of a prestigious research department – a Guardian Good Father client of mine – that Nell was just the person for the challenge in programming that was opening up in one of his teams. This seasoned band of colleagues were taking on a high-profile task at the leading edge of technology and there was a hole in their skill set. Nell was duly invited to join the team on the basis of her reputation in the area where a focused expertise was required. The project manager – a Hero Warrior type – was keen to get his new recruit embedded into the team quickly and so asked everyone to be sure to make her welcome in every possible way. In typical Hero mode, he wanted Nell to 'hit the ground running' so no time was lost in getting the project underway. This Hero manager was full of good intent, but his rushed and pushing strategy was counterproductive.

In Centaur terms, Nell is a perfect example of a Magical Sprite. Perhaps you remember that the unconscious worldview of the Magical is:

- *I am fragile.*
- *Others can be hostile.*
- *The world is dangerous.*

With this worldview writ deep within their unconscious minds, Magicals need space and time to adjust to change and they are uneasy with interpersonal contact in the best of circumstances. Is it any surprise that lots of people enthusiastically inviting her to lunch and after-work drinks in her first week was something of a nightmare for Nell? She felt overwhelmed by all the attention that came her way, however well meant it was.

Inwardly, she froze in apprehension and, outwardly, she withdrew from contact, fleeing to her office and closing the door. To her new colleagues, Nell appeared distant and aloof. Her lack of positive response to their offers hurt their feelings and offended their pride. Putting Nell's behaviour together with her impressive reputation, caused some to conclude Nell was arrogant and saw herself as better than them. As a result of these negative conclusions, some of the team drew back from contact, creating exactly the hostile atmosphere that Nell unconsciously expected from others. Obviously this was not a good start for collegial relationships and a good team spirit. It got worse.

Because she felt ill at ease, Nell avoided the interactive culture for which the team was well known. Moreover, her growing tension curbed her creative flow which, combined with her lack of collaboration with colleagues, led to a stalling of the project. When I was invited to take Nell on to my coaching schedule, her new boss was questioning the head of department as to whether it had been a mistake to bring Nell into the team. I was called in by the Guardian head of department to advise. On hearing the narrative and seeing photographs of all involved I had a clear sense of what had occurred and how I might help.

By good fortune, a team away event was scheduled in the next weeks and I suggested that on those days we run the Centaur training workshop that had been scheduled for later in the year. In this programme each character type is described in terms of the gift they bring to any situation along with what they struggle with in terms of expressing their potential. Each member of the team is helped to identify their Centaur type along with those of their teammates. The second principle of Centaur work – that others can be different from me and still valid – is the major learning for all. Having established the proposition that every person has a resource of untapped potential within, the developmental story behind each personality type is recounted in detail. This results in real insight into what lies behind everyday behaviour in the different types. This process is exciting for individuals as they identify their natural gifts and clarify their growing edge. It also leads to a deepened understanding of what happens within the dynamic of the team.

I had met with Nell before the workshop to give her a head start on the material and help her understand why things had gone so badly for her on arrival into the team. She was gratified to see her personality so clearly described in the Magical Wizard/Sprite category. She also saw how she might help herself and others in the 'threshold' moments where Magicals tend to freeze and withdraw.

During our discussion she came to see how her fearful reactions caused her to be misunderstood. She realized that her defensive behaviour had hurt and offended her new team. Within the safe context of the workshop Nell was able to make a fresh start with her new colleagues. From the vantage point of the Centaur framework, team members were able to understand Nell's reactions to their well-intended but rushed approaches. As often happens in these team-building events, they agreed on a playful signal that would facilitate relaxation – which is the key to interactive creativity. If Nell felt contact was getting too intense she was to make a 'time out' sign with her hands, which would mean she needed space to think things through or just to take a breath.

The workshop experience saved Nell's future in the team, and it also cleared up a number of interpersonal 'glitches' between other team members as they came to know one another in more depth. Centaur became helpfully installed in their daily language. When they resumed work on their challenging project the next week, all felt grounded and inspired.

A Brief Look at the Formative Years

A sense of how memory works and evolves is helpful in understanding the ways in which differing worldviews and therefore different personalities develop in the course of the formative years.

Developmental psychologists suggest a sequence of human capacities that unfold during these important early years. Neuroscientists confirm that at each of these junctures new capacities come online in the brain. Each capacity requires the right relational 'crucible' in which to flourish both psychologically and in terms of brain development.

Simplified, these could be seen as a series of 'rights' that must be respected as the baby moves through critical stages to become a 'reason-able' child at the age of five. These five rights of the formative years frame the sections on personality types in Chapter Two. They are described in brief below.

Five Rights of the Formative Years and Their Wholesome Conclusions

At five distinct stages during the formative years, new issues and capacities emerge in the development of a child. Two are in babyhood, and a third of great importance emerges during toddlerhood. A final two unfold between three and five years old once a child has the brain capacity to think rationally and so becomes a 'reason-able' child.

How these successive needs and rights are responded to by parents determines the shape of attitudes toward self, others and the world that form a worldview. These stages with their concomitant rights are listed below along with the wholesome attitudes that will be wired into a child's brain if the social context is wholesome and supportive.

The Right to Exist: first six months
If this right is respected the child concludes:

- *I am safe.*
- *Others are on my side.*
- *The world is a good place.*

The Right to Nourishment: first year
If this right is respected the child concludes:

- *I can make things happen.*
- *Others respond to my needs.*
- *The world is exciting and stimulating.*

The Right to Power: one to two and a half years
If this right is respected the child concludes:

- *I have a right to affect the world.*
- *There are others in the world and they also have rights.*
- *The world must be shared with others*

The Right to Freedom: two to four years
If this right is respected the child concludes:

- *I am free to adventure.*
- *I can express myself even if others disagree.*
- *The world responds to my passion without pushing it down.*

The Right to Love: four to six years
If this right is respected the child concludes:

- *I am free to love.*

- *I can compete and measure myself against others without sacrificing love.*

- *The world is a place of adventure where I can define myself.*

When a formative right is not sufficiently respected at any of these five junctures the resulting worldview will reflect the mismatch between the child's needs and the response of its parental environment.

The players in our introductory case study provide examples of five distinct wounds. A closer look at the formative history of each of the five types follows in the next chapter.

How About That 'Totally Ethical Unfair Advantage'?

Having established how a worldview is formed in the mind and brain of a growing child, we will now explore the basis for the most unusual offering of the Centaur approach: how aspects of the physical body reflect the attitudes of mind that compose the worldview.

This body-mind connection discovered by Freud's star student Wilhelm Reich will allow you to literally 'read' the mental orientation of individuals you encounter by noting aspects of their physical structure and posture. Reading the body in this way – called here 'soma reading' – will allow you to quickly assess and then respond to others in a manner that is attuned and respectful. Such interactions lead to good outcomes. A discussion of the all-important body-mind connection follows.

REICH AND NEUROSCIENCE
The Body Mirrors the Mind

Wilhelm Reich followed in the wake of Freud, and for a time was his crown prince within the growing kingdom of psychoanalysis. Most remarkably, Reich expanded the Freudian notion of the unconscious mind by extending its reach into the physical structure of the body. In his long career working with therapy clients, Reich observed that individuals with particular body shapes and postures tended to have comparable life attitudes and that, in addition, they were inclined to recount similar childhood histories.[6]

On the basis of these observations, Reich proposed that during the formative years not only the mind, but also the body responds to and is shaped by interactions between parents and child. Finding that the worldview held by his clients appeared to be *mirrored* in aspects of body shape, Reich proposed that personality is not just a matter of mind, it is a body-mind.

It is not the whole of the body nor all of the mind that are linked in this way. Much of our body form is inherited and determined by the genes we receive from our parents. Nevertheless, Reich and his followers maintained that etched upon this genetic base are readable patterns of physical tension that affect the shape of the body and reflect fundamental attitudes of our unconscious worldview.

Reich's unique contention was that – with a trained eye – you can read a person's core attitudes from patterns of tension in their body. What I am calling 'soma reading' provides the most remarkable and practical gift of the Centaur approach to leaders and managers. With this skill you can look at a person and know – often within seconds – what they value and how they think.

With Centaur there is no need for a long interview with a time-consuming questionnaire. A focused glance through the Centaur lens provides clues on how best to motivate, influence and inspire the person in front of you.

As with Freud, recent findings in neuroscience appear to support Reich's notion: that the body and the mind develop simultaneously in response to family context and that – explicitly and concretely – they mirror each other. This validating research will be discussed shortly.

The notion that aspects of our physical bodies reflect inner attitudes of mind is a hard step for many. But over the past three decades, thousands of Centaur delegates and coaches have found it to be both true and deeply helpful.

Five Holding Patterns Underpin Five Personality Types

These networks of physical tension are called 'holding patterns'. Five such holding patterns were identified by Reichian protégées Alexander Lowen and John Pierrakos.[7]

These are pictured and named below:

The black lines indicate networks of entrenched muscular tension that shape the body and mirror unconscious attitudes of mind.

As a result, each of these has a distinct physical look, which corresponds to a worldview. In this way, with an attuned gaze, we can know how another person thinks by paying attention to their physical form.

This is not the 'body language', which was so popular in the 1980s and remains useful still. Body *language* focuses on fleeting gesture and posture to reveal a person's mood and inclination *in the moment*. In the Centaur model the term 'soma reading' is used to describe the discernment of these more permanent patterns of muscular tension in the body that reflect the abiding attitudes of mind, which in turn shape the way we react to others and to life.

Such insight is extremely helpful in leadership and managerial work. With this awareness you can know in a moment how to motivate members of your team, devise a considered approach that will influence those above you and think strategically about how to handle important and/or difficult clients.

The 'mindful management' of others is the most practical application of the Centaur model and thousands of leadership and sales professionals have put it to the test over the past three decades, achieving excellent results. In Chapter Two the 'mindful management' of colleagues and clients is specifically highlighted.

REICH'S BODY-MIND, BIOENERGETICS AND NEUROSCIENCE

In New York City in the 1950s, Reich met and trained two young American doctors – the aforementioned Lowen and Pierrakos – who consolidated the body-mind approach into a robust therapeutic model which they called 'Bioenergetics'. With Bioenergetics the idea of the body-mind was refined and different personality forms were correlated with particular events in the formative years of a child's development.

Thousands of clients passed through the doors of the Bioenergetic Institute in New York City over the decades and their stories, along with their therapeutic progress, were recorded and studied. This data formed the basis of hypotheses regarding both causation and treatment. These hypotheses were tested and sufficiently proven, providing the basis for this practical and effective therapeutic mode. Bioenergetics underpins the typology offered in the Centaur model. In Centaur this therapeutic approach has been translated into the language of everyday life useful to managers and leaders in the world of business.

Reich and his followers would have felt validated by current research findings in neuroscience, which highlight, through hard evidence, the connections between physical form, psychological orientation and formative context in childhood. Both Siegel and van der Kolk report that the quality of the relationship between baby and caregiver can affect the literal growth and development of physical structures in the brain.[2 and 5]

A heartbreaking example of this connection between environmental deficit and structural distortion is revealed in studies recounted by Siegel of the effect of babyhood stress on the growth of the hippocampus (that vitally important part of the brain described above that translates implicit memory into explicit awareness).[2]

In response to early experience of fright and/or neglect, the amygdala alarm system sets off the fear circuits within the brain and powerful hormones – adrenalin, noradrenalin and, worst of all, cortisol – flood the baby's system. This biochemical surge has a devastating impact on the emerging hippocampus: growth is literally and measurably stunted and the developmental capacities it should offer are compromised. Researchers record quantified shrinkage in the hippocampi of traumatized children and observe psychological difficulties as they go forward in life.[5]

An extension of this concrete impact on a structure in the brain to impact on the body in general is made easy by the remarkable revelation that your brain and your body proper are, in fact, all one system. We will explore this remarkable notion by continuing a discussion of the two cortical hemispheres of the brain, focusing first on how spectacularly different they are from each other.

Differences Between the Left Brain and Right Brain

Previously the triune nature of the brain was discussed in order to explain how an unconscious worldview is formed within the memory wiring of our limbic system. It was proposed that, from this unconscious level of the brain, orientating attitudes of mind – concluded during our formative years – affect how we think, feel and behave in everyday life. In a way the limbic system could be seen as the physical location of Freud's unconscious mind.

Now we are about to uncover a similar metaphorical correspondence between another physical location in the brain and the Reichian body-mind.

At the level of the neocortex our three-part brain divides into two discrete halves, which are frequently referred to as the 'left' and the 'right' brains. These two halves of the brain are vastly different from one another. For a start, the left and right brains are strikingly asymmetrical. Even though the same subcortical structures appear in each hemisphere, they are radically different in both size and in the activities they perform.

For example, there is an amygdala on both the left and the right sides, but it is significantly smaller on the left, reflecting the less emotional, more cognitive and logical character of the left brain. Other sub-cortical structures on the left also have more specifically rational functions. Language, for example, is primarily a feature of the left brain where it operates in a particularly 'left brain' manner to describe specific and concrete aspects of the world.

The operation of the left side of the neocortex corresponds most closely to Freud's conscious mind. Your conscious mind (your left brain) is composed of what you are aware of and can put in logical, rational, sequential order and communicate through language. Neurobiologist Dan Siegel helpfully relates the qualities of the left brain to the letter 'L'. The left brain, he says, is *logical*, *linear* and uses *language*. It also tends to be quite *literal* in comparison with the poetic and emotional propensity of the right brain, much of which operates *out* of consciousness.[2]

Through the lenses of our new technology we know that the left hemisphere of the brain lights up and comes 'online' when a child begins to talk sometime between the second and third year of life. This represents the tiny beginnings of the capacity that will come to fruition between three and five years of age in the 'reason-able' child.

I often ask parents in my classroom to disclose at what age they were able to make a functionally successful 'deal' with their child. Something like 'If you will stop screaming here in the grocery store I will give you an ice cream when we get home.' Typically, around three years of age is the answer given. This deal-making capacity indicates that the function of the left brain is coming online at a predictable moment and in an expected manner. By comparison, the right brain is active from birth and, as previously suggested, even before birth.

The Body as Part of the Right Brain

The left brain is conventionally contained within the skull and is, in fact, virtually separate from the right hemisphere. All that connects the two hemispheres is a network of delicate fibres called the corpus callosum, which provide a modest conduit between these two totally diverse domains. To get the measure of your left brain, cup your hand around the left side of your head. You are literally holding your left brain.

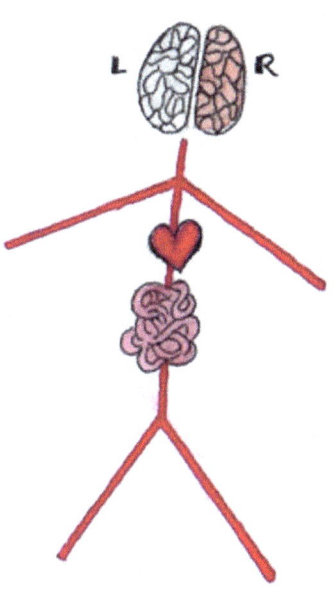

Your right brain, by comparison, reaches beyond the skull down into the body proper via the powerful processes of the brain stem in which it is rooted. The asymmetry of the left and right brains is pictured here.

Daniel Siegel offers us a fitting new definition suggesting that the word 'brain' refers to '… the distributed nervous system throughout the whole of the body'. From this perspective, the function of your brain is not limited to the grey matter that sits within your skull; it is an extended network made up of comprehensive neural connections that run throughout the body and this 'body brain' connects solely into the right hemisphere of the skull brain. This huge neural system is what is referred to as the 'right brain'.[2]

So, the right brain unfurls throughout the entire body via these extensive neural connections that link all of our vital organs to the nervous system collected inside the skull. To get a feel of the vastness of your right brain, put one hand on the top of the right side of your head and then run your other hand down your chest and over your belly and below. This is your right brain. I am suggesting that this right brain is equivalent to Reich's body-mind.

A Brain in the Gut and a Brain in the Heart

A two-fold aspect of the brain called the autonomic nervous system projects from the right hemisphere down into the major organs of the body. One branch – the sympathetic system – is like an accelerator. The other – the parasympathetic branch – is like a brake. Our heart rate, our digestive juices and our breathing are all influenced by this system that runs from the skull down into the deep organ systems and into the musculature of our bodies, revving us up for action or calming us down into a state of equilibrium.

Amazingly, there is an extensive network of identical neurons to those found in the skull brain located within our intestines and another similar network distributed around our hearts. Neuroscientists call these 'parallel-distributed processors' (PDPs) and these PDPs in the body have been shown to be able to process information in a very complex way. *This means that we literally have a brain in our intestines and a brain in our hearts that is in every way comparable to the brain in our skulls.*[2]

The PDPs around our intestines and our hearts give us the 'gut feel' of a situation or a 'heartfelt' reaction to another person. It would seem that the guiding wisdom of intuition and the tender sense of meaning spoken of by poets are not just literary metaphors. They are actual organic happenings based on chartable neuronal mechanisms within our body-brain.

Neuroscience and Reich's Body-Mind

Reich's contention that events in the formative years of a child can shape the physical structures of the body is arguably supported by the neurological findings discussed above. For example, when the amygdala reacts in a fright response releasing cascades of stress hormones, that biochemical 'surge' will not be limited to the skull brain. It will course through the entire body including the muscular system. It makes sense that these other aspects of the physical system will also be affected.

Reich studied the structure of the muscular system rather than that of the brain, but the principle is the same. What happens to the child during the uniquely massive growth period of the formative years is bound to affect both the structures within brain and body's muscular system.

The body-mind link made by Reich and his followers is accessible to the naked eye in aspects of muscular tone and tension. It is these observable reflections of the mind in patterns in the body that are so helpful in tuning into other people.

In the Practical Application chapter that follows, aspects of physical form will be shown to signal specific personality types – each with their characteristic worldview – allowing you to know at a glance how another person thinks and feels about themselves, others and the world.

It is this ability to read the mind from the body that gives you that 'totally ethical unfair advantage' for which Centaur is famous.

How Does the Body Come to Mirror the Mind?

The physical shape that identifies each Centaur type is created by a pattern of muscular tension that emerges in response to the need to diminish and block unwanted feelings that occur in the life of the growing child. These patterns are superimposed upon our inherited biological data, and they have an effect on the shape and posture of the body.

It is important to remember that energetic 'soma reading' is concerned with muscular blocking patterns that develop during the formative years, not with genetic data that is present from birth. The Centaur focus is solely concerned with the 'nurture' side of the nature-nurture divide. Your 'nature' or inborn temperament constitutes the psychological heritage carried in your genes. It is a very important aspect of who you are and most experts suggest that it is largely unchangeable.

Centaur, on the other hand, is concerned with the worldview that we gather as we make our journey through the early years of life. Answers to the questions: 'Who am I?' 'What is the nature of others?' and 'How does the world work?' are *learned* through experience. Unlike our genetic temperament, our worldview is most definitely changeable. Anything we learn we can *unlearn*. Change is certainly possible within the Centaur domain through an 'examined life' and a commitment to work on our body-mind or personality.

Each personality type is created around the management of a particular feeling. Put simply, at a given stage within the formative years, the child must handle feelings that cause pain. Each character form has a definitive feeling at its core that reflects the formative crucible of its worldview. Our five types are based on five big feelings: fear, sadness, shame, anger and heartbreak. In Chapter Two the manner in which these feelings shape personality will be explored in detail.

In phenomenological terms, a feeling is a *movement* within our physical felt sense. We typically say 'I was *moved* to anger or to tears' or 'my joy transported me (moved me) into another world'. Imagine that various core feelings *move in different channels* through your body and that each major feeling has a unique pathway. We acknowledge this directionality of emotion in the way we speak about feelings every day. Here are some key examples:

Joy

Joy surges up from the heart, knocking the head back and lifting the arms in its expression. Picture the triumphant gesture of an Olympic winner or a football player scoring a crucial goal. We say *'my heart leapt for joy'*, *'I'm over the moon'* or *'walking on air'* or *'high as a kite'*.

Sadness

We know intuitively that disappointment or sadness travels down the soft front of the body, an awareness reflected in the expression of disappointment like *'my heart sank'*, *'I am feeling down'* or *'the bottom fell out of my world'*.

Fear

Fear raises the shoulders and widens the eyes in the classic startle response. When we are frightened, we say *'I nearly jumped out of my skin'*.

Anger

Anger, on the other hand, rushes up the backbone, cresting over the shoulders and is expressed into the world with forceful movements through the arms, a blaze in the eyes and a strong sound in the throat like a shout or a growl. We say our *'blood is up'* or our *'hackles rise'*.

The anger pathway is plainly visible in animals. A cat arches its back as its fury moves up and into expression when it faces your dog, and the fur between the shoulder blades of your dog bristles and stands up when its aggression is aroused in response.

Acknowledging feeling as energetic movement within the body is central to understanding body-mind psychology and how it can be helpful in Centaur's soma reading, which reveals the worldview of others through looking at patterns of tension that shape their bodies.

A second critical notion is that a feeling must 'move' in order to register and be experienced consciously. If a person stops the energetic movement of a feeling in their body, that feeling may not register in awareness. In this way someone can *be* very angry yet not *feel* that anger at all. This is an unwholesome and even dangerous situation. Being unaware of our inner emotional landscape to this extent is unhealthy and would definitely call for a 'an examination' of how such a life is being lived – or rather how it is *not* being lived.

Of course, all of us on occasion must stop the flow of our feelings because of professional or social requirements. A board director may be utterly furious with his chairman during a meeting, but he will be wise to *hold* that feeling until a later moment where he can express it appropriately and safely.

A candidate for a promotion may feel a sob of heartbreak move in her chest when she learns that she has been unsuccessful, but she will hold back the expression of her disappointment until she is privately at home. It is important to be *aware* of when we do this and shortly after to find ways of 'processing' those held feelings appropriately.

For example, a vigorous workout in the gym is a good way to discharge anger arising from a frustrating day at work. Likewise, a heart-to-heart talk with a friend is a healthy way to release feelings of disappointment or sadness. Feelings that stay 'held' for a longer time in the body become toxic, causing strain and in due course stress, draining our vitality and undermining our resilience.

The everyday – and hopefully conscious – holding of feelings away from expression is an 'acute' necessity in social and professional living. This is very different from the 'chronic' and unconscious holding patterns that define the Centaur types. These originate in childhood, they are unconscious and their grip limits and distorts how we think and how fully we live. Becoming aware of these patterns gives us the *choice* to make changes and positive *change* opens up the *opportunity* to live a larger life.

How We Block Our Feelings Bioenergetically

Whether chronic or acute, there are two ways that we stop or diminish our experience of feelings. Both can be demonstrated by calling to mind common everyday events. If you bash your finger with a hammer when hanging a picture on the wall or stub your little toe while rushing to get ready for work, there are two spontaneous reactions which occur even before you swear or cry out:

1. You tense your muscles.
2. You hold your breath.

Both of these actions reduce the experience of pain caused by your mismanagement of your hand or foot.

This example highlights the two key energetic processes through which feeling is controlled spontaneously in the service of comfort. First, the movement of a feeling is diminished or even halted by tensing muscles and so closing or constricting its channel of movement. If a feeling does not move, it will not reach consciousness. The holding patterns that underpin each Centaur personality type are composed of networks of muscular tension that stop the movement of feeling.

Secondly, limiting breathing will reduce the strength of a feeling. Feelings are like fire, both need air to flourish and grow. If you want to enjoy more of a positive feeling, all you need do is take a deep breath. This will be like applying a bellows to a fire – the feeling will increase. The opposite is also true. If you starve a feeling or a fire of air both will lose their vividness and die away.

Have you noticed how shallow your breathing becomes when you are afraid? Fear is uncomfortable and starving it of breath lessens its impact. Likewise, anger management coaches train people who are given to explosive outbursts to 'hold their breath and count to ten' thereby reducing the intensity of the feeling, thus making it manageable.

In summary then, the energetic understanding of feeling is based on two premises which underpin the process of soma reading:

1. *Feelings are movements within the body* rather than mental events. Specific feelings have 'directions of movement' or 'channels' which distinguish them from one another.

2. *Feelings must move in order to be felt.* This movement can be limited and even stopped by tensing relevant muscle groups and holding the breath.

Any muscle that is used repeatedly for whatever reason will grow in strength and volume and so take on a recognizable shape. For example, the serving arm of a professional tennis player is notably bigger and stronger because its musculature has been used regularly for a specific purpose. In the same way as a tennis player's serving arm grows larger and more defined from repeated use, a readable muscular geometry emerges as individuals employ various sets of muscles to block specific feeling channels during early life. When muscles are used habitually to control feelings they form 'energetic holding patterns', which are readable and reflect attitudes of mind. Through the skill of soma reading the body can be seen to mirror the mind.

How We Develop a Habitual Response

There are two reasons why human beings block feelings. The emotion may be painful in and of itself or social pressure may make us uncomfortable with it. Fear is physically painful and when allowed full expression, it can be utterly disorganizing. We need to restrict the flow of fear in order to take defensive action. Unchecked fear can threaten our chances of survival and so human beings are 'hardwired' to block fear.

This hardwiring is not a learned reaction nor is it culturally variable. If a loud BANG sounds anywhere on the planet, all within earshot will react with what is known as the 'startle response': eyes widen, shoulders draw up and together and necks draws in.

In terms of our evolution it was crucial to human survival that fear be blocked and held away from expression. When someone is overwhelmed by fear in a war movie or a film about dinosaurs we intuitively *know* they are a 'goner'. When a character's capacity to 'hold' his fear is overthrown and he panics and dashes around out of control, we are not surprised when he (depending on the movie) gets mown down by enemy gunfire or becomes the dinosaur's dinner.

In the classic startle response fear is blocked by holding the breath and clenching in all joints.

When a person blocks fear habitually over a lifetime, shoulders will become chronically high and square and appear fragile rather than strong. It is as if this individual has been frozen in the startle response. As will be revealed, the look and geometry of shoulders which block fear are different from those that block anger or hurt. The various shapes created by patterns of holding in shoulders are examples of the physical clues to soma reading that will help you discern the personality type – and the concomitant worldview – of the person in front of you.

Early experiences have led our 'frozen' individual to conclude that 'the world is a dangerous place'. High fragile shoulders which are blocking fear indicate a Magical (Wizard/Sprite) personality type. A psychological characteristic of people with shoulders like these is a predisposition toward wariness, even paranoia. Extra care must be taken when interacting with them to ensure that their unconscious fear does not 'project' onto the present situation and cause problems for themselves or you or others. Wizard Sam in our introductory case study contends with chronic fear. When given what his Hero manager felt was a reasonable challenge, Sam's chronically held fear was triggered and he became stressed and therefore less effective.

By comparison to debilitating fear, the emotion of anger is empowering and it can focus the mind. The pain of anger is not in the energetic charge itself but in the social reactions to it. For example, within some families it is judged as bad, unloving or even sinful to be angry. In this case the discomfort with anger and the associated impulse to block it is *learned* rather than *organic* as is the case with fear. The blocking of anger is 'soft wired' rather than 'hardwired' in human beings. All people experience the startle response, only some block anger. In both cases, however, a person controls the unwanted feeling by tensing certain muscle groups, thereby closing the channel of expression. In this way the unwanted emotion is held away from expression, or even from awareness altogether.

The shoulders of individuals who block anger have a very different – and equally distinctive – shape from those that block fear.

The shoulder muscles that block anger are massive and strong from the ongoing effort of closing the anger channel. The overall form of these shoulders is rounded and strong with considerable mass and volume. They turn downward and pull forward, literally putting a lid on aggressive passion, which surges up the back and seeks expression through the arms, eyes and voice.

This physical shape mirrors the attitude 'anger is bad, it damages relationships'. This is the developmental story of the Centaur Guardian type, the Good Father and Earth Mother. Typically, the family of individuals with these shoulders will include strong parental messages to 'hold in' anger rather than express it into the world of others. 'Be good, behave, be nice', 'Don't get too big for your britches!' and above all 'Don't show off!' are familiar instructions whether said or unsaid. Shoulders like those pictured here – along with other specific characteristics like proportion, facial shape and quality of gaze – indicate a personality with the Guardian worldview, where dedication to responsibility and courtesy to others predominates. As in the response of George in our case study, Guardians can be trusted to do the task and they will typically respect authority. However, they probably *will not* tell you directly when they are angry with you and may, as a result, harbour grudges and can move into modes of passive aggression. Typically, Guardians find it difficult to speak out in disagreement, especially to figures of authority. Most particularly, it is hard for them to say 'no' because their personality is organized to avoid conflict and to prioritize others over themselves.

Hopefully, it is clear from these two examples that the muscles used to block fear are different from those used to block anger and that the chronic holding of these separate muscle groups produces distinct and readable patterns that mirror very different attitudes of mind.

In each of the five Centaur types a muscular pattern reflects key attitudes that may be the source of behaviours which other personality types find hard to understand. Learning to read the body of another can be of enormous help when dealing with someone who thinks very differently from you. Detailed descriptions of the body-mind patterns of each of the five types follow in the next chapter.

In Summary

During the first five years of life – those Freud named 'formative' – massive growth occurs both physically and mentally, far more than in any other period of our lives. Physically, a five-year-old is *five times* the size of a baby and experts who chart mental development claim that during these years our brains absorb *more than half* of what we will learn in our entire lives.

During this fecund time, a child concludes which aspects of its nature are acceptable within its family context and unconsciously blocks those aspects which are not in line with family culture. Fundamental attitudes are established mentally and physically and strong muscular contractions stop the expression of unwanted feelings, creating a distinct and readable physical pattern. These patterns of tension mirror primary attitudes toward self, others and the world at large. In this way, shapes in the body that are visible to an educated eye reflect mental orientations. Muscle literally mirrors mind.

Each of the five basic personality types to be described here has a core feeling which is chronically blocked and an attendant set of attitudes, which reflect their basic dilemma. Once this physical language is understood it is possible to know at a glance who needs a cautious approach where another will respond well to a challenge, how best to handle a low achiever or motivate a disenchanted team member, why certain clients and colleagues are difficult and what they need in order to give of their best.

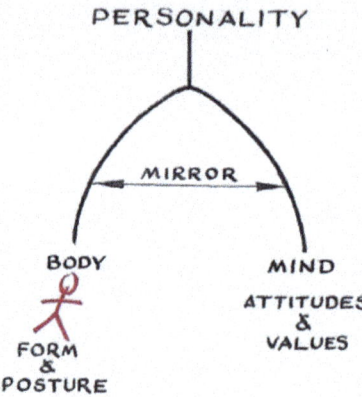

With this information, leaders and managers can plan an approach to others in the service of mutual success.

JUNG AND COMPLEXITY THEORY
An Organizing Principle Within

To begin with a review: the ideas of Freud, Reich and Bioenergetics all focus on interpersonal events within the formative years in answering the question 'Who do you think you are?' All are based on a cause and effect model. We enter life a *tabula rasa* – a blank sheet – and there is absolutely nothing in the human mind until it is put there by experiences with other people. Events occur between the child and others and those events etch formative memories deep within the limbic 'wiring' of the child's psyche.

When we interact with important others early on we 'constellate' orientating attitudes toward life based on the feelings that arise from these interactions.

When we manage and control these feelings by holding our breath and tensing our muscles, a pattern of physical tension is created simultaneously that reflects these fundamental attitudes of mind. Both Freud's unconscious worldview and Reich's body-mind are forged early on in interaction with parents and family. In this picture our personality is 'all we are' and that personality is solely the product of the experiences with important others in the first few years of our lives.

Carl Jung and those who followed his thinking acknowledge the importance of the formation of personality during childhood.

However, they do not buy into the idea that we are born a 'blank sheet'. In this view, there is more to you than you think and, moreover, it is positive.

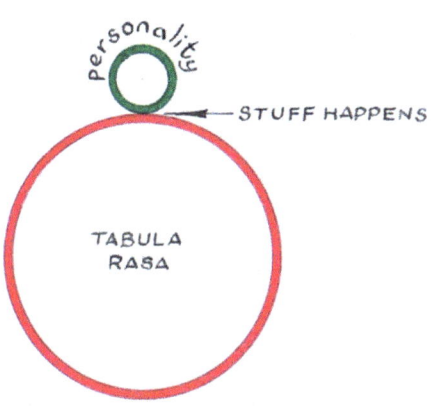

Jung's theory of the human mind proposes an organizing principle deep within the psyche that *underpins* every human personality in the same way as our physical skeleton forms the basis of our physical bodies. According to Jung we do not enter life a blank sheet. There is a deep structural layer within each of us which contains *potentials and principles common to all people*. This wider and deeper domain of the unconscious is of a different order than Freud's personal unconscious, which is the result of repressed experiences from the formative years. Jung's unconscious is inborn and present from the very start of life.[8]

At the core of this deeper aspect is what Jung called the 'SELF', written with capital letters here to designate its importance and distinguish it from the 'personality self' that is gathered during the formative years. Jung maintained that this SELF deep within seeks to guide the personality self in its way-of-being-in-the-world throughout the unfolding stages of a lifetime.

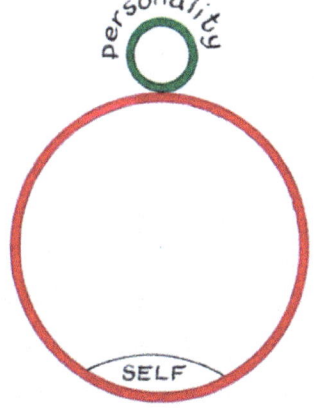

The question is, can we, as personalities, tune into the messages of this SELF within? Might this attending to something deep inside of us be the process Socrates was indicating when he recommended the 'examined life'?

Freud and Jung were contemporaries and for a while close friends, but it is clear that their ideas about the make-up of human nature were radically different from each other. These differences eventually caused a rupture in their friendship.

In current language we could say that Freud was dedicated to the 'left-brain' method of 'testing and proof'. Like many in the early 20th century, Freud was empirically minded and aspired to a scientific validation for his theories.

By comparison, Jung looked to mystical traditions and esoteric religions for guidance, and his ideas reflect those of philosophers like Socrates, Plato, Hegel and Kant. In all of these, a 'right-brain' intuition proposes an innate code of virtue at the very core of being human.

Through this lens each of us possesses an inner sense of what Plato called the 'Good' and religious scholars refer to as a 'Spark of the Divine'. More contemporary thinkers use the term 'moral compass'. All of these suggest that natural ethics is present in all of us from our very beginning. Within this larger perspective there is more to 'who we are' than the formative collection of experiences – or personality – proposed by Freud and those who followed him. We are moral beings from the very start.

The Idea of Destiny

According to Jungian thinking we enter life with a *purpose* in both our personal and professional domains.[Ibid]

The SELF, located in the depth of the unconscious mind, houses the 'code' or key to this purpose, which Jung called our 'destiny'. Your destiny is *who you are meant to be*. For Jung, a healthy psychological life is one where we live out who we are meant to be in the outer world of others. We will feel satisfied and fulfilled when we manifest the life that is *destined* within us.

Have you ever felt magnetically pulled toward a field of study, deeply curious about a topic or lost in contemplation of a landscape or a painting? At moments like these Jung suggested that we are communing with our deep SELF and he maintained that it is wholesome to stay open to this vital inner connection and to value and seek guidance from such happenings.

At other times, when we feel out of sorts, ill at ease, depressed or disheartened it is likewise important to ponder questions as to 'why that is', and not settle for easy answers that blame other people or outer circumstances.

The deep SELF within constantly sends signals to the personality self. Some people become aware of their destiny early on in life through a powerful intuitive experience that captures their imagination. For example, the famous chef Heston Blumenthal recalls a luminous moment approaching a magically alight restaurant with his parents as a young boy. He reports that in that moment he realized he would be a chef. Likewise, the painter, Paul Klee exclaimed on seeing a range of luminous and brilliant colours, 'now I am a painter!'

The SELF deep within constantly sends signals to our personality self, letting us know when we are moving in the right direction and where we are going off track. When the dialogue between the 'deep SELF' and the 'personality self' goes well, an individual grows into the person they are meant to be. Jung called this the process of 'individuation'. The fruitful SELF-to-self dialogue lies at the core of healthy and inspired living.

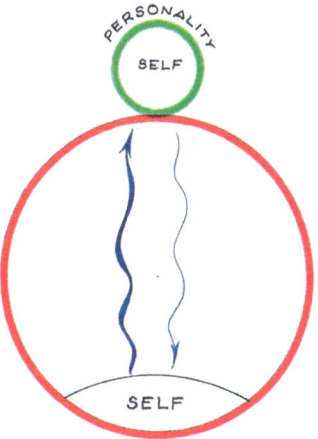

Alas, there is frequently a mismatch between the 'directions' (of our destiny) from within and the 'demands' (during the formative years) from the outside world. I recall a poignant scene in a medical drama on TV where an exhausted junior doctor and a jaded nurse sat together sharing their mutual dislike of their profession, which it turned out had been chosen for them by their respective families rather than arising out of their own desires.

'I was always great at golf as a kid,' the young doctor shared, 'and I dreamed of going professional and making my living with my golf. But that would never do in my family.' He went on to explain, 'We are all doctors in my tribe from my great-grandfather who was that loved country village doctor, through my medically famous grandfather to my equally famous father right down the line to me. So, here I am.' He sighed and repeated, 'Here I am.' Then – with a second and deeper sigh – he reported, 'Oh look, there is a little piece of poo on my trouser leg.'

'I always wanted to be a hairdresser,' confided his equally exhausted companion, 'but my mother told me it would be a sin to pledge my life to vanity. So here I am sticking needles in and emptying out bedpans…' and her words and gaze faded away. It was a wistfully beautiful little scene featuring two lost souls confiding in one another about how enervating it is to live somebody else's idea of what your life should be.

In Jungian terms, the junior doctor and the jaded nurse had had their lives hijacked by family pressure into a life pattern Jung might call 'healer', when they were *inwardly called* to the paths of 'athlete' and 'artist' respectively.

The Collective Unconscious

Jung taught that – along with a guiding SELF – people enter life with an inner collection or catalogue of human potentials and possibilities inscribed in full within the deepest reaches of the unconscious mind.[Ibid]

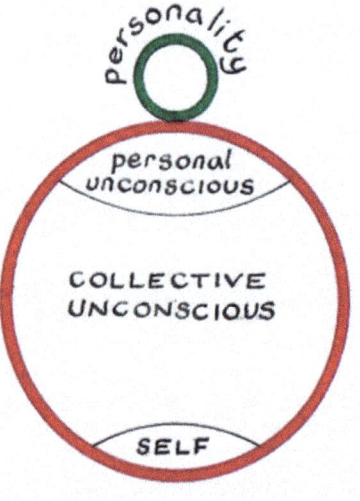

The image here pictures the Jungian 'Collective Unconscious' in conjunction with the Freudian personal unconscious showing how the two together give a layered and nuanced sense of who we are.

The Freudian unconscious is *personal* to each of us, containing repressed memories from our personal history that were too painful to tolerate. The early wounds at the core of these repressed memories are the source of the limiting attitudes and physical tension that diminish and distort how we live our lives today.

The healing intent of Freudian-based psychotherapy is to bring such memories into consciousness and then – as a grown person and with the help of an analyst or therapist – come to terms with them.

By comparison, Jung's 'Collective Unconscious' is not personal. It is universal. It sits at a deeper level within the psyche than Freud's personal unconscious and its contents have never been conscious. Nevertheless, they exert an influence on the shape and quality of our lives. Within this Collective Unconscious are all of the patterns of 'being' and 'relating' that our species has accumulated over thousands of years of human history. These collective memories – etched deep within that archaic layer of the unconscious mind – form mental patterns that are shared by all human beings, forming a common imagination that lives within each of us.

'The Collective Unconscious,' Jung wrote, 'contains the whole spiritual heritage of mankind's evolution, born anew in the brain structure of every individual.'[9] Jung maintained that all religious narratives, myths and folk tales arise out of this profound, inherited 'wiring' and that they represent, in essence, a 'projection' of the Collective Unconscious into accessible stories that we can be guided by when making choices in our everyday lives. Jungian psychotherapy seeks to help individuals connect with these deep collective characters and storylines in order to imagine our futures and take meaning from life's hardships and so live expanded and enriched lives.

In conceiving his ideas of the Collective Unconscious Jung was influenced by the studies of the early 20th century explorer and archaeologist Adolf Bastian who travelled the world studying the way different peoples live and structure their societies. Bastian was amazed to find that wherever he went he found the same basic stories and motifs in cultures that were vastly distant from one another in time and location. Everywhere there are instances of 'creation myths', 'virgin births', 'hero saviours', 'devastating floods' and 'predictions of the world ending' all with the same storyline and in many the exact same trajectory and ending. On the personal level, there is in every culture 'a wise old man', 'a great mother', 'the wicked witch' along with her nicer sister, 'the fairy godmother' and many more. The names differ but the essence is the same all over the world.

Bastian called these recurring motifs 'elemental ideas' and he maintained that they represent eternal themes lodged deep within the human imagination. In a way, the Collective Unconscious is like the 'limbic system of the psyche' of the human race. It houses the foundational memories of our species over thousands of years and as such it carries within it all *potential* ways of 'being' and 'being together' along with certain deep principles – the Golden Rule for example – which have energized human imagination down through the ages.

Jung named Bastian's elemental ideas 'archetypes' and he proposed that these innate patterns within provide us with templates of how we might live in the world as individuals. The Centaur personality types are all examples of archetypes – the Wizard, the Damsel, Superman, the Earth Mother, the Warrior and the rest – which call to mind images that are easily accessible within the realm of our imagination.

We have already explored how three of these archetypal patterns – 'Healer', 'Athlete' and 'Artist' – can relate to everyday lives in the previous story of the young doctor and the disheartened nurse. In this story, both of the protagonists felt the 'call' of their destiny during their childhood. The young doctor was drawn by the 'Athlete' exemplified by his golfing talent; the nurse, by the 'Artist' in her fascination with designing hairstyles. Both were taken off course by social forces in the outer world of family traditions and judgments. This is not to say that every whim of childhood ought to be given archetypal importance. If that were the case, the world would be full of 'firemen' and 'princesses'. Nevertheless, good parents look for soulful desires and talents in their children and take them into account. These 'callings' are the source of vitality and pleasure so crucial to a vivid living of life. We need only revisit the depressed and disengaged relationship that the young doctor and the jaded nurse had to their imposed professions to sense the cost of their derailment.

Joseph Campbell was a brilliant Jungian-inspired author and lecturer who spent his career teaching bright and privileged young women at the Sarah Lawrence College in New England in the United States. In his classes on philosophy and mythology Campbell ignited much excitement in his pupils, telling them how every one of us is on a 'hero's journey' in the living of our life and that our everyday experiences mirror – in however small a way – the dilemmas and choices featured in the stories and legends of classical mythology and religious history. In his classroom he encouraged his students to pay attention to their 'inner voice', passionately supporting their 'individuation' with the exhortation to 'Follow your bliss!'

If you learn to use your imagination to discover 'which myth you are in', you can find solace and guidance in these storylines that have fascinated and educated people for thousands of years. I found this to be true at a critical turning point in my own life.

In an earlier section describing how memory is formed, I recounted a wonderful moment with a much-loved partner where his declaration of love for me on holiday in Scotland fused with flowering red rhododendrons causing the latter to become an unconscious trigger for feelings of delight and happiness.

I spent some of the richest years of my life with that partner, but, sadly, a savage midlife crisis hit him at age fifty causing our relationship to fall apart. This is a far from unusual happening in the world of couples. Midlife (once associated with age forty but now anchored quite firmly at age fifty) represents a significant turning point for us all with its powerful invitations to transformation and deepening.

In the course of his middle passage, my treasured partner fell out of love with himself and his life and I was part of the latter. As a result, he left our relationship to engage in a brave and harrowing inner journey searching for an authentic way of being within the new life stage unfolding before him.

Countless classic tales recount the landscapes and dramas of the journey of midlife, with their descriptions of feeling lost and at sea in the midst of confusing and daunting forces. Dante's *Inferno* begins with one of the clearest descriptions of the onset of the midlife ordeal:

> *Midway upon the journey of our life*
> *I found myself within a forest dark,*
> *For the straightforward pathway had been lost.*

Canto 1 *Inferno*, Dante Alighieri

My partner totally identified with the description above. But it was Homer's *Odyssey*, which recounts the journey of the hero Ulysses in his adventure to find his way back home from the Trojan War, that helped me with my heartbreak and loss. I found an identity with Penelope – wife and queen of Ulysses – who waited patiently for her husband's return.

Underneath the sadness and anger that always accompanies the rupture of relationship, I felt a patient belief that all would be well and I found the example of Penelope helpful and reassuring. While she waited, Penelope conducted her life with dignity and creativity and as a result, with the close of the ordeal, she too had grown in stature.

This good and brave man did return to me – albeit as a dear friend rather than a partner – and we agree that we have both changed and grown as a result of these difficult times. Myths and stories provide containers for the turbulent and confusing feelings that accompany transformation and change. They allow us to see our lives through a lens that focuses on a sense of agency and heroic adventure rather than on helplessness and victimhood.

Jung taught that our 'destiny' is composed of a collection of 'archetypes' or potentials, which each of us is *meant to live out* in our lifetime. For example, all of us will have inhabited the archetype of 'Son' or 'Daughter' and many readers will be living out 'Father' or 'Mother' and some of you will be within the archetype of 'Husband' or 'Wife' in a 'Marriage'.

I frequently witness the power of archetypes when friends who have lived together as sexual partners for years decide at last to marry. Often they are a little shy about this decision, finding it somewhat embarrassing because they have no *rational* explanation as to 'why now?' Of course I think I know why. The ritual of marriage signifies the archetypal promise of two people to live together throughout a lifetime in fidelity and trust.

The couples I refer to have done just that and it makes poignant sense to me that they inwardly yearn for their accomplishment to be acknowledged – sanctified actually – in the presence of others whom they also love. Typically, they say, 'It won't make any difference to us really.' Then, often they are amazed at how touched and moved they become during the ceremony and how different they feel when they are, in fact, married. Archetypes are powerful forces in human life and we are enriched when we acknowledge and respect them and we ignore them at the serious risk of shallow living.

Being in touch with your inner voice and open to your destiny does not necessarily mean things are easy. Archetypes are demanding and can be in conflict with one another, sometimes causing disruption and discomfort to the 'hero within' on his or her committed journey. Let me tell you a story to illustrate this point.

I have a niece – Jannie – who is only ten years younger than me and so she is more like a 'Sister' than a niece. 'Sister' is a primary archetype, so when I identify Jannie as my 'Sister' I indicate that the relationship between us is of a different importance and intensity than that typical between a niece and an aunt. Because she is my 'Sister', I have always been close to Jannie's life and very interested in her decisions. When she turned thirty Jannie hit the classic female dilemma of career vs motherhood.

At that time something occurred that taught me about archetypes and how they work in our everyday lives. Jannie and I were out Christmas shopping that year and she was enthusiastically sharing that she was choosing the call of leadership over the idea of motherhood as she entered her next decade. She had discussed all this with her husband and they were agreed on the plan for the next five years. Indeed, Jannie's career was going marvellously well and I was as excited as she when I heard about her possibilities.

Now, let me pause my narrative here to prepare readers for the twist in this tale. Every Christmas in America there is always a fabulous 'toy gimmick' that captures everyone's imagination. This particular year it was a big, irresistibly darling teddy bear that had a heart beat that pulsed when you held him to your chest. Not being in the market for toys neither Jannie nor I knew about this bear. In the midst of telling me of her career aspirations, Jannie randomly picked up one of these teddies and hugged it tightly to her saying, 'Oh, isn't he cute!'

As she put the bear to her chest, a tiny other 'heart' suddenly beat next to hers. I watched in amazement as my dear 'Leader-Sister' paused, then softened and melted. Her body relaxed and her eyes filled with the sweetest of tears. We were both speechless for some time. Neither of us knew in that moment quite what was happening.

On reflection I believe I saw the 'Mother' archetype ('Demeter' in classical mythology) challenge 'Athena' (the classical 'Leader Queen') for the starring role on Jannie's inner stage. The tiny heartbeat triggered a change within her that was waiting to happen. By the following Christmas Jannie, indeed, had the wonderful job she told me about while shopping the year before and she also had a darling baby daughter in her arms.

Without her conscious 'permission', Jannie's process of 'individuation' had stepped up a gear and she found herself engaged in that challenging balancing act which characterizes the lives of many courageous young women who serve both Demeter (the Mother) and Athena (the Queen).

Jannie's story illustrates how the personality self – whether it knows it or not – is subject to the demands of the archetypes of the Collective Unconscious and the influence of the deep SELF. The image here illustrates these connections.

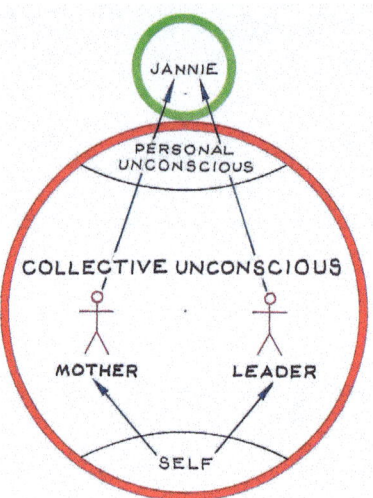

The archetypes of Mother/Father and King/Queen represent the 'parent' and 'leader' patterns respectively. Each of these extends into larger relationships. The parent pattern presupposes 'Marriage' and leads to the 'Child', while the leader path implies team patterns like 'Band of Brothers' and 'Sisterhood'. Both of these sibling-based team patterns are typical of the Hero (Warrior/Huntress) personality type. Guardian leaders, on the other hand, tend to run their teams as a 'Family', taking a leadership role akin to a protective and nurturing parent. In Chapter Two we will discuss in more detail how personality types relate to particular archetypal patterns in their inner values and leadership styles.

In psychologically healthy people like my niece, there is an open connection between the personality self and the deep SELF. Such individuals can 'examine' the lives they live against an inner code of rightness, which they intuitively sense, as Jannie did in her response to that unexpected heartbeat while hugging the teddy bear.

The image above shows how messages and guidance, suggestions and requirements flow from the deep SELF to the self-in-the-world, enabling the personality to expand, flourish and flower into a life fully lived. As mentioned previously, Jung coined that term 'individuation' to describe this process of becoming who you truly are through this SELF-to-self dialogue.

Two questions follow on this image: 1) Will the 'personality' we have constructed during our formative years be able to connect to the deeper psychic forces and resources within? And 2) if it does connect, will the personality form be strong and flexible enough to provide an adequate channel into the world of others for *who we are meant to be*? The Centaur approach provides helpful guidance regarding both of these questions.

The Importance of Ego Strength

How well we can *function and operate* in the world and *make things happen* is a crucially important feature of our personality self, and it is vital to successful SELF expression. 'Ego' is the name given to this capacity for agency or 'getting things done'. Your ego is a central aspect of your personality.

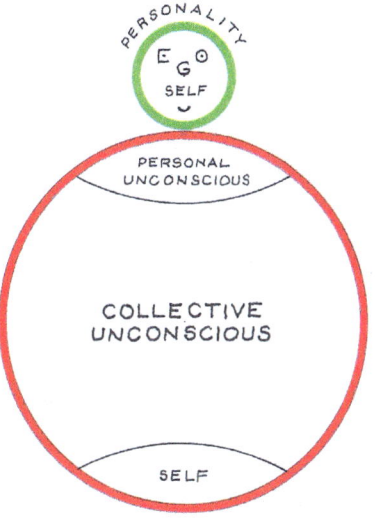

It is important to have a robust and resilient ego in place like the one pictured here so you can deal with both the outer world of other people and your inner world of potential. If we are guided by Socrates and 'examine our lives', seeking to become who we are meant to be then it will be the ego aspect of our personality that will express our inner truth into the outer world.

The strength, resilience and flexibility of ego function differs from personality to personality. A problematic ego can be variously 'fragile', 'weak', 'inflated', 'squashed' or 'rigid'. In the chapter on practical application that follows, an image denoting the ego form of each of the Centaur types will graphically illustrate important differences in the ego strength of the five personality types when compared to this ideal.

The Centaur approach is designed to help individuals develop and improve 'ego strength' in order to 'individuate' and so live their full potential in the world of others. The journey toward a strong, grounded, flexible and expressive way of being in the world is a key goal in Centaur work.

The Jungian SELF and the Science of Complexity Theory

There is a satisfying reassurance in finding that discoveries in the field of neuroscience in recent decades appear to support, even validate, the classical thinking of Freud and Reich. A confluence between the theories of these great scholars of the human mind and the hard empirical science of brain research consolidates and adds to both.

Jungian ideas find no correspondence in empirically focused neuroscience. However, Jung might well have recognized a reflection of his thinking in the mathematically based notions of Complexity Theory, which currently rivals neuroscience for a place in popular fascination. Unlike concrete, observation-based neuroscience, mathematics embraces the non-tangible and abstract in search of overarching principles that lie behind what we concretely observe.

I am not mathematically inclined, and so I rely on neuropsychologist Daniel Siegel's simple and helpful translation of the notion of Complex Systems into psychological terms in order to link this Jungian level to current ideas in science.[2]

What is a Complex System?

A 'complex system' is defined by three characteristics. Looking through the Centaur lens based on Freud, Reich and Jung, it is clear that human beings most definitely belong to this category, as will be explained below.

The First Characteristic of a Complex System:
A complex system is multilayered and these layers are often in opposition to and disrupted by one another. The usual illustration for complexity theory is the formation of clouds where molecules of water and sunlight along with other aspects of atmosphere such as wind interact to create the unpredictable emergence of weather systems.

As we have seen, human beings are also composed of layers that converge, clash and disrupt, creating an emergent and changing edge to our existence. Think of the battle between the conscious and the unconscious mind catalogued by Freud. In Nancy's story, for example, we saw how her conscious, competent self was overthrown by deep, old patterns in her unconscious mind.

In discussing Reichian bioenergetics we described how our feeling flow can be blocked and held away from expression by patterns of muscular tension in our bodies. For example, an energetic flow of anger will surge up the backbone seeking expression through a punch or an angry hand gesture, a harsh sound in the voice and hard look in the eye. But, if the personality is anger averse, the muscular system will clamp down on that flow. Strong shoulder muscles will 'put a lid' on the rising passion so that it remains unexpressed.

In Jungian thinking, rival archetypes struggle for prominence. Remember my niece Jannie's dilemma as her inner Demeter or 'Mother' archetype pushed against her inner Athena, the archetype of the female 'Leader'. Moreover, the deeper SELF may use disruptive tactics to intervene and instruct a personality self that has gone out of balance or off track. Think of the poignant pop lyric by Macy Gray that describes what happens when the singer's ego wants to go against the deeper wishes of her heart.

> *I try to say goodbye and I choke*
> *I try to walk away and I stumble*
> *Though I try to hide it, it's clear*
> *My world crumbles when you are not here*

Neuroscience parallels and concretizes some of these clashing systems, charting the different processes of the left and right brains, implicit and explicit memory systems and rational and intuitive processing of information. All that was presented in this chapter confirms that a human being is a perfect illustration for this first aspect of a complex system.

The Second Characteristic of a Complex System:

Complex systems are open to and affected by other complex systems. Again human beings fulfil this requirement. We are interactive and relational creatures. Initially our very survival and eventually the quality of our development (including the literal development of the structures of our brains) are dependent on interaction with others.

In the world of clouds, different weather systems meet each other and outcomes are contingent on unpredictable interactions between them. Human beings are likewise open to other (human) complex systems and when we meet we impact and affect each other, just as weather systems do. As with weather systems, any number of differing outcomes are possible at the meeting of two people. Think back to the introductory case study. Hero Peter interacted with four other complex human systems and in each case a different interpersonal scenario unfolded.

Unlike weather systems, human beings can *think* and *plan*. How we choose to approach another person (another complex system) can potentially bring out the best of who they are, lead to their personal development or produce a good business outcome. Alternatively, how we approach another can cause them to contract and go on the defensive, refusing to cooperate or to buy.

It is at this kind of 'edge' that a leader, colleague or sales professional meets those s/he hopes to inspire, motivate or influence. This is where the Centaur approach can be a helpful guide. The manner in which this 'edge between us' is best navigated with regard to each personality type is described in detail in the next chapter in the section entitled 'Mindful Management'.

The Third Characteristic of a Complex System:

This third and most amazing aspect of a complex system arguably invites comparison with the Jungian SELF. Of this singular quality Dan Siegel writes, 'There is something inherent in the way the components (of a complex system) interact with each other that leads to a self-organizational flow across time.'[2]

In Complexity Theory this innate organizing principle propels complex systems toward an ideal state which, when achieved, theoretical scientists call 'elegance'. At the core of this abstract theory of the workings of the universe is the notion of an inner orientation toward balance and order that to my mind is reminiscent of the intention of the deep SELF within a human life.

I was surprised and delighted to find that within the cool domain of science a subjective and emotional term like 'elegance' is given such prominence. The confluence of this theory of self-organization leading to 'elegance' in all of nature and Jung's idea of the SELF guiding a human life toward 'individuation' seems to me both arguable and obvious.

How This Applies to You and Me

In each of our lives what disrupts a SELF-organized flow are the distorting attitudes that arise from 'misses' in our social context during our formative years. The limitations of our personality can make it more or less unfit for the purpose of expressing who we truly are.

For example, how can a young woman fulfil a 'leadership' destiny that is based in the archetype of 'Queen' if she has grown up in a household that instructed little girls to be only 'sugar and spice and all things nice'? Such phrases are rarely said out loud these days, but the cultural attitude that spawned them still holds sway more than any of us would like to think. Moreover, silent disapproval is often more powerful and effective in dampening down self-expression than direct confrontation in any case. The Guardian personality that gives us the loving Earth Mothers and supportive Good Fathers emerges from a formative crucible that actively says or silently vibes 'be good, behave, be nice – don't upset others.'

Such a context will 'wire in' a negative attitude toward speaking her mind in our aspiring Queen and limit or even block the flow of assertion in her body. The successful expression of the leadership archetype relies on the free flow of assertion and passion and the willingness to challenge others at the risk of possible disapproval. As we will see in the next chapter, deep discomfort with the disapproval of others, most especially of authority figures, is characteristic of the Guardian personality. Our young Earth Mother who is destined to be a Leader Queen will have some development work to do if she is to live her life to the full. Centaur can set her on her way. In Chapter Two suggestions for focused self-development are outlined in detail for each type.

When an individual corrects limiting attitudes of mind s/he will, as a matter of course, become increasingly conscious of which archetypes are waiting in the wings for expression. New vitality and a sense of dedication are sure signs of connecting to these deeper directional forces in our being. When aspects of attitude and destiny become aligned, the organizing principle of the SELF can guide a human 'complex system' through 'individuation' toward the 'elegance' of a fulfilled life.

The Centaur Model Now Complete

With our discussion of the Jungian deep SELF we have all the ingredients that compose the Centaur approach. There are two key principles in Centaur work. The first and most important comes from Jung and the ideas just explored.

The first and *most central* principle of Centaur is: **There is more to you than you think and it is positive.**

In the chapter that follows, limiting attitudes that keep you away from fulfilling your true potential – your destiny – will be explored and ways to get beyond their grip outlined.

The second Centaur principle is based in the ideas of Freud and Reichian-inspired bioenergetics. This most practical aspect of Centaur will give that 'totally ethical unfair advantage' when dealing with the fact that: **Others can be very different from you and still valid.**

Chapter Two provides insight into the workings of others that will help you approach them personally and professionally in ways that will lead to resilient relationships, successful interactions and inspired leadership.

Notes

1 Gay, P. (1988) *Freud: A Life for Our Time* London: J.M. Dent & Sons Ltd.
2 Siegel, D. (2008) *The Neurobiology of We* Audio Book. Boulder: Sounds True
3 Schore, A. (2009) *Relational Trauma and the Developing Right Brain* New York: Academy of Sciences
4 Bowlby, J. (1969) *Attachment and Loss*: *Volume One* London: Penguin Group
5 Van der Kolk B. (2014) *The Body Keeps the Score* New York: Penguin Books
6 Reich, W. (1945) *Character Analysis* (Third Edition 1972) New York: Doubleday
7 Lowen, A. (1975) *Bioenergetics* New York: Penguin
8 Storr, A. (1998) *The Essential Jung* London: Fontana Press
9 Jung, C. (1970) *The Structure and Dynamics of the Psyche*: *Vol 8*, 2nd Edition (Collected Works)

CHAPTER TWO: Practical Application

PERSPECTIVES

Before beginning this focused discussion of the Centaur model, I would like to frame it within a wider context. My overarching view of a human being is captured in the image of a multifaceted, multidimensional diamond. Did you know that in the world of concrete diamonds, the quality of a particular stone is judged on how many of the facets align with – or point to – its core? Imagine that in my metaphorical diamond this core is the 'truth' of our human being. Then it is clear that there are many facets of, or windows into, 'who we are' and expressions of 'how we are' in the world.

The Centaur body-mind types represent only one of these many facets.

Another really crucial aspect is the genetically transmitted psychology that we inherit from our parents. An orientation toward being 'introvert' or 'extrovert' is an example of this inherited 'temperament', along with attributes of being a so-called 'hot' or 'cold' responder or whether one is 'shy' or 'bold' interpersonally. Our individual temperament is present at birth and remains a constant throughout life. Anyone who has taken the excellent Meyers-Briggs Type Indicator (MBTI) multiple choice test – or any of its follow-on incarnations – will have had an indication of their inherited temperament.

Unlike temperament, Centaur personality forms are not present at birth. As described previously, they represent the attitudinal framework or 'worldview' that we unconsciously formulate during the first five or six years of life in our interaction with important others. In a way, temperament can be seen as a 'hardwired' aspect of our way of being. It is there from our inception and typically does not alter throughout our lives. Because our temperament does not change, we might be well advised to make our social life and our career choices around it in order to avoid the stress of 'going against our grain'.

A Centaur type, on the other hand, is 'soft wired' into our psyche during our early childhood. The core attitudes of the Centaur worldview are *learned* and *anything we learn, we can unlearn*. Moreover, as some of our core attitudes 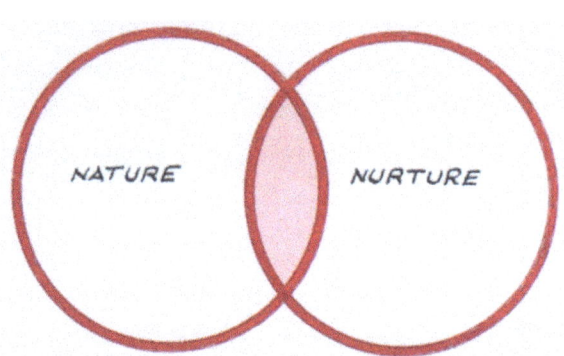 limit our potential, we are well advised to challenge and amend aspects of how we view ourselves, others and the world so we can live larger and richer lives. Therefore, although Centaur represents only one of many facets of who we are, it offers a particularly dynamic lever into self-understanding and personal development.

This distinction between inherited temperament and learned worldview recalls the once fierce debate between 'nature' and 'nurture' in terms of what determines who we are in the world. For decades in the past, thinkers and researchers lined up in stark opposition, each side laying out highly articulate claims to sole responsibility for who we are. That is all changed now. Although there are still some stubborn encampments maintaining that all is determined by genetics, most concur that both inherited temperament (nature) *and* learned worldview (nurture) are more or less equal factors in our creation; a ratio of 60 per cent of one and 40 per cent of the other is generally agreed. From a binary dispute of all or nothing, most of us have come to a somewhat amicable squabble over 10 per cent or 20 per cent.

There are other important facets in our 'human diamond' that play into how each of us expresses ourselves in the world. All of these other facets mitigate and ameliorate our Centaur presentation. For example, whatever our Centaur type, gender has an impact on how we express ourselves in the world and so do social mores and the dictates of our culture.

A biochemical gender basis in testosterone as opposed to oxytocin and oestrogen arguably predisposes men under stress to active risk and women to a protective enfolding of others. Even when they share the same Centaur type, men and women will differ in their responses to challenging situations.

Likewise, socially – even in the liberated west – what is 'allowed' women in terms of aggressive/assertive expression is different from that which is seen as okay for men. And alternatively, it is acceptable for women to be more tearfully emotional than it is for men to express their tender feelings openly.

Finally, different cultures lay down strict rules that will constrain assertive expression even when that energy flow is organically free within the body of an individual. In the Centaur 'Hero' type, for example, assertion is unrestrained in the body-mind system. In the U.S. outright expression of assertion in straight-talking and direct gaze is culturally acceptable and will likely be a valued interaction with a boss. In India, on the other hand, this would be regarded as disrespectful and unacceptable. In Asian culture, the eyes of a junior avoid direct contact with those of a more senior person as a matter of respect. In Asia not meeting the gaze of one's boss may be seen as appropriate and good. In the U.S. it would be read as 'shifty' and 'untrustworthy'.

These are the most important 'other facets' that affect how we present ourselves in the world. There are additional ones that are less central but nonetheless interesting. I briefly alluded to Bowlby's 'attachment styles' earlier. Another one of these concerns the impact of birth order. Research shows that being born first or last or in the middle often has an effect on personality. Generally speaking, first borns tend to be more responsible and serious. The 'baby' of the family is more playful, less competitive and resists growing up, while kids 'in the middle' tend to be a little 'lost' in one way or another. The diamond image here captures

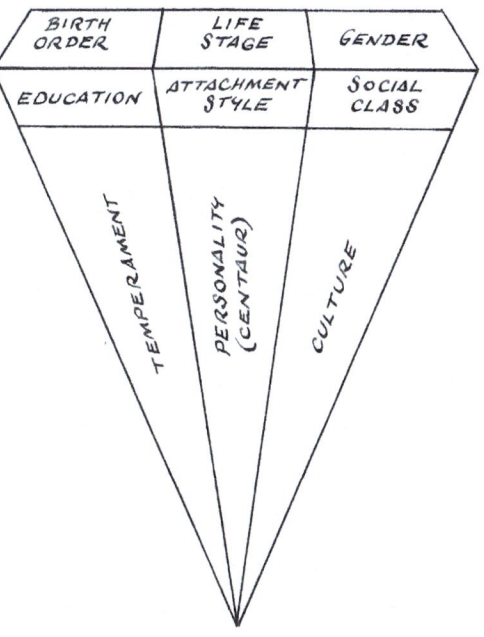

these different influences on our way of being in the world. We humans are, indeed, 'complex systems' composed of different layers and processes that interact and disrupt one another in our journey into being.

Having established that Centaur is but a single facet of who we are, this chapter aims to show that it provides a genuine key to unlocking both personal potential and interpersonal effectiveness.

Shortly we will explore in detail the sequence of unfolding that developmental psychologists propose, tracing the journey from babyhood through the toddler phase to the status of a child who is able to think in a reasoned way when entering school at five or six years old.

These stages will be connected to the five Centaur personality types in order to provide insight into yourself and others.

Studies of the brain by researchers like Siegel, Shore and van der Kolk confirm that psychological tasks of maturation correspond to specific structures and functions that emerge in the developing brain. The unfolding of the triune or three-part structure of the human brain broadly reflects the three chapters in the story of the formative years: the baby, the toddler and the 'reason-able' child.

As we will discover, what forms personality are instances of relational mishap or wounding at one or another of the developmental stages. Something happens that is not in line with the child's genetic and archetypal expectation and as a result, s/he is disrupted and wounded. In defensive response a life-limiting attitude is 'wired in' that is geared to ensure the hurt does not happen again. At the same time, the breath is held and the body braces in order to subdue the painful emotion caused by the interpersonal 'miss' with the important other. This is how a body-mind pattern emerges.

This body-mind structure is created to protect; however – because it is unconscious – it lingers on after the causative factor has long gone, diminishing the sparkle available for living life. In this way vitality and potential has been foreclosed in every one of us.

The good news is that when we become aware of limiting attitudes, we can examine them through our conscious mind and change the way we think and therefore how we live. Likewise, targeted 'body work' can complement and enhance these changes of mind. It is entirely possible to heal wounds from the past and these healing changes of mind and body enable us to express more of our potential.

Guidance on 'self-development' for each Centaur type follows within each of the sections on the five personalities. Moreover, as managers and leaders – and also as colleagues and friends – when we provide the right context for others, we can support their growth and enhance their development. Suggestions for the 'mindful management' of each character type conclude each section.

In our introductory case study, manager Peter lacked the necessary flexibility in his approach to the different members of his team and, with nothing but goodwill in his heart, he made harmful mistakes with most of them. It is a core requirement of good leadership to develop and bring forth the potential of others. Ideas of how to do exactly this are simplified and codified in the chapter sections referred to above.

THREE BASIC NOTIONS IN PSYCHOLOGY

Three helpful psychological notions will provide a basis for our in-depth discussion of Centaur's body-mind personality types. These are: 'good enough parenting', 'assumed reality' and 'optimal frustration'.

Good Enough Parenting

I worry when I begin to teach my students – who are typically parents – about the formative years. I sense dread in the classroom and can almost 'see' a collective thought bubble emerge above their heads that says, 'Oh no! Now I am going to hear how I have totally failed my children.' I try to ameliorate that fear by introducing them to the notion of the 'good enough parent' given to us by the wonderful British psychoanalyst Donald Winnicott. In the 1950s Winnicott went on the radio to encourage mothers to trust their natural intuition in raising their children. He reassuringly maintained that you do not have to be a perfect mother or father to raise a psychologically healthy child.[1]

Human beings are actually quite resilient creatures and so long as needs are 'pretty much' met and the inevitable 'misses' not too extreme, a well-functioning version of one of the types will hatch into the world at around six years of age. Moreover, events quite outside of the domain of parental failure can and will affect the personality development of a child. Parents are helpless in the face of traumatic external events like war or natural disasters that create a stressful atmosphere that can affect a child. Within the more intimate sphere of the family, there may be financial constraints that mean one or both parents must be absent more than they would wish to be. Above all, parents cannot control unwelcome crisis at birth or in the physical health of their child throughout the formative years. Such things happen and they do have an effect on personality formation. Good enough parenting provides a helpful buffer against external threats and ensures subsequent healing contexts following such misadventures in babyhood and early childhood.

Assumed Reality

It is not always what actually happens that affects the growth and development of personality. It is what the child *assumes* is happening. A baby may be born to parents who are devoted and loving, but if the birth is traumatic or if there is a babyhood illness that requires invasive treatment the experience will not *feel* loving and so the *assumed reality* will be one of alienation and fright. When the crisis has passed, the reality of the loving context will soften this original 'misconception' but this child may retain a 'fright circuit' at the implicit level of memory, which will have an effect on how the world is perceived unconsciously. This could easily be the history of Wizard Sam in the introductory case study. As will be discussed in detail shortly, each personality type has a 'gift' that – paradoxically – is the result of the unwanted wound in the formative years. This wound is also the source of an individual's 'developmental issue'. The good news is that – unlike genetic temperament – the attitudes of mind that underpin personality *can be changed* and the original wounding healed. As mentioned previously, a roadmap to self-development of each type is included in the following discussions.

Optimal Frustration

The development of ego function in human personality is similar to muscle development in a person seeking to become fit. In a way, the ego is the 'muscle function' of the personality. It gets things done. In both a muscle and an ego, strength is built by dealing with *optimal* pressure. For example, if I want to enhance my biceps, I will lift weights that put pressure on the muscles of my upper arms. I literally 'frustrate' the intended lifting in the exercise by the heaviness of the weight. If the weight is too light and therefore does not sufficiently 'frustrate' the lifting, my muscle tone will not improve. On the other hand, if I try to lift a weight that is over heavy, I will damage myself.

The same principle applies in the building of ego strength. The frustration must be 'optimal' or the ego will remain undeveloped or be damaged. Moreover, what frustration is optimal changes as a child grows. When a newborn signals for comfort or nurture, 'optimal frustration' will be to get that nurture or comfort to the baby as soon as you can. This tiny creature has just come from in utero where there was no such thing as 'cold', or 'hungry' or 'alone'. For the first time ever s/he must 'sing for their supper', that is, signal to the outside world in order to get an inner need met. If the pressure of waiting is too much, damage may be done.

However, if two and a half years later you respond to your *toddler's* needs with the same committed alacrity that is correct for a newborn, you will be building an inflated and entitled ego form that lacks a realistic view of self and others. At the toddler stage learning to tolerate 'waiting' through appropriate and optimal frustration is crucial for healthy ego growth. At this stage, children learn to say the 'magic word'(please) and behave appropriately in order to get what is wanted. This pressure of waiting is a crucial aspect of the socialization process, which leads to living successfully with others. Psychologists call this particular kind of waiting 'delayed gratification'. Most of us can think of adults we know or have known who clearly missed the 'optimal frustration' necessary to be able to tolerate waiting their turn or not getting their own way.

THE CHARACTER CONTINUUM: POTENTIAL NOT PATHOLOGY

The Centaur Model is based on the therapeutic system of bioenergetics developed in the l960s by Lowen and Pierrakos. However, because Centaur was developed specifically to work with managers as opposed to therapy clients the language and examples have a different tone to therapy-based description and case studies.[2]

Psychotherapists serve people who are having difficulty making a workable success of their lives. Good therapy is a brave and committed attempt to heal what is broken and make good the life at hand.

Our students are managers – a population which is by and large psychologically robust and what psychologists call 'high functioning'. The nature of managerial work requires a strong sense of self and a resilient ego. The vast majority of our students have made sound lives for themselves and their families. However, there is always work that can be done and more human potential to access and enjoy. We address the same kinds of personalities as psychotherapists but our corporate clients are typically stronger and more resilient. Therefore, within the bioenergetic typology a *quantitative* as well as a *qualitative* dimension exists. Qualitatively, our work mirrors that of therapists.

Quantitatively, Centaur clients require much less time to achieve positive change in the way they live and work in the world.

Psychologist Stephen Johnson helpfully describes a continuum of functioning, ranging from healthy or high functioning, which he calls 'character style' through a functioning dysfunction, which he calls 'neurotic' to the total dysfunction of 'character disorder'.[3]

It is along this continuum that a decisive difference between managers and those who typically seek long-term psychotherapy exists. Managers tend to be 'character style' while long-term therapy patients may be 'neurotic' or even more extreme.

A character style is a healthy workable mode of personality *in any of the five types*. If character or personality were a wheel, a character style would be round and full and capable of rolling along successfully albeit in different shapes reflecting the particular *quality* of the personality type.

A neurotic patterning is more deeply entrenched, more life-limiting, characterized by more disturbed behaviour. The neurotic wheel would have a warped rim and would sometimes lurch unpredictably or roll out of control.

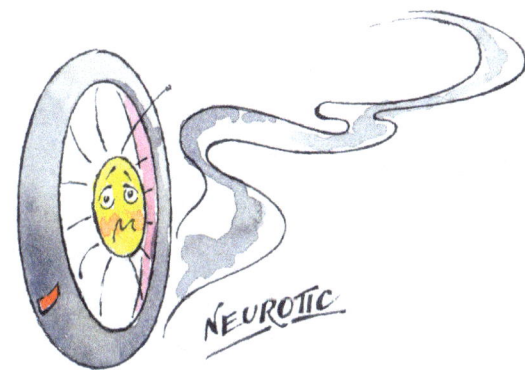

This metaphor is a good one. Human personality like a distorted wheel can be worked on so that its function improves.

If a 'character disorder' were a wheel, it might be a flat tyre with a broken rim. Forward, reliable, predictable movement is not possible without a lot of attention and repair. Individuals with such a deep body-mind limitation will not be seen in managerial life. Depending on their personality type, they will be found in hospital or in jail or – sometimes in the superhero category – at the head of a rogue nation!

The Centaur model describes character style manifestations based on Lowen's five types. Archetypal titles – by now familiar to the reader – replace the pathological labels used by Lowen, which are necessary within the field of therapy. In the following descriptions of the character types examples of the darker, or shadow, side of the archetype are included in order to give balance and scope to the discussion.

THE DEVELOPMENTAL STORY

STAGE ONE OF DEVELOPMENT
BABYHOOD: The Crucible of Magicals and Romantics

The task of the infant is first to survive the transition from the safety of the womb to the world of separate people. Once parted physically from the mother, the newborn must crucially reconnect to her by establishing a psychological bond of nurture and love. Of course, a caregiver other than the baby's mother can act in this capacity. For simplicity I will use 'mother' or 'mother figure' to indicate this role, whoever may fill it.

When neuroscientists like Allan Schore and Dan Siegel observe the brain of an infant through MRI technology, much of it is 'dark' and inactive. Alight are only those aspects that support, first of all, essential aliveness and secondly – and of equal importance – those that promote basic connectedness. The brain structures that support essential aliveness are located in the brain stem. Here are those crucial fundamentals like heart rate, blood pressure and fight/flight responses along with sleep patterns that provide a basis for life.

But in order to survive a *human* baby needs more than basic aliveness. S/he must *connect*. The limbic system – the seat of emotions – is alight and active even before birth. All mammals have a warm-blooded need to bond to a 'mother' and build an emotional as well as a biological relationship with her. Crucial to the well-being of all mammals is a sense of a safe and secure attachment to another human being. A confident worldview, which includes a robust sense of self and a positive expectation of others in the world, depends on this kind of good beginning.[4, 5]

Ideally, a baby feels s/he is the absolute centre of a world that is adoring and responsive. Nature provides for this in maternal hormones that make the newborn the 'primary preoccupation' of a mother who is biochemically attuned to the particular cry of her own child along with various other nuances of sound that can come from that precious bundle. In such a context the infant feels safe, breathes easily and the growth hormones spring into action while the neurons in the brain wire up a positive worldview. We are meant to orbit our young in a state of loving trance. *Babies are supposed to be babied* – that is, cherished and protected. When they are not, there will be sad repercussions in later life. Two of the Centaur personalities are formed in babyhood: the Magical and the Romantic.

A benign 'illusion of grandiosity' is the desired context for a helpless infant who, in reality, has no power whatsoever. The last thing we want is for babies to realize the truth of their situation: totally helpless and utterly at risk. Failure to install a secure sense of safety in babyhood leads to particular challenges later in life. In our players from the case study Wizard Sam's orientating attitude, 'I am fragile' and Damsel Julie's conviction, 'I am in need' reflect issues in babyhood.

In the context of a generous and safe babyhood, a confident worldview emerges:

- *I am precious.*
- *Others are loving.*
- *The world is good.*

THE MAGICALS: The Wizard and the Sprite

This personality type is created around the Right to Exist, which is formative during the first six months of life.

The Developmental Crucible of the Magical

It is not possible for grown-up, worldly-wise people to imagine the innocence and openness of a human being in babyhood. Experience impacts directly and is registered at the implicit level of the brain. Memories composed of feelings, images and interactions are clustered together in non-rational associations that will rest below the level of consciousness and affect the perceptions of life hereafter. Existence at this stage is totally sensual. All is either warm or cold, soft or hard, rough or smooth, alive or still, full or empty. Moreover, whatever state is present at this moment is eternal. There is no past or future, only the eternal 'now'. The memories that form at this first stage of life lay down a basis on which all others are layered. A good, safe, generous babyhood creates a strong and optimistic foundation for life.

Having been for all time in the utterly sensual and totally contactful container of the womb, a seismic change happens with the process of birth. The quality of the birthing event and the experience of life that immediately follows gives rise to our most deeply held attitudes and assumptions.

The first of our formative crucibles occurs in the initial six months of life when the Magical Wizard/Sprite pattern is formed. All of us would agree that a new baby has the right to be loved and welcomed into the world. The joy in our hearts at the news of a healthy birth and our delight at seeing a new baby are spontaneous and organic affirmations of this truth. The way a newborn experiences this welcome is through contact. The pleasurable touch of warm skin against warm skin along with the sunny radiance of a loving gaze relaxes the infant into a new post-womb experience of ease and pleasure.

The little body reaches for contact and upon receiving it, bonds with the caregiver. A positive physical intimacy between mother and child is crucial to the development of an abiding sense of self-value, along with a confident and hopeful expectation of others and the world. A newborn experiences who s/he is by the way s/he feels. If s/he *feels* good, s/he *is* good. If s/he does not feel good, more negative conclusions begin to form. Psychology and physiology are one at this stage, where our most foundational sense of self and self-esteem are established.

The Magical pattern results when a human newborn first senses and then assumes – correctly or incorrectly – that s/he is not welcome and concludes that s/he has no right to existence.

The very worst case is when a child is actually and actively not wanted. Babies can be unwelcome from the start as with some unplanned pregnancies or parents may think they want a child until the reality of the unrelenting needs and demands of a totally dependent being turns their lives upside down. Real infants are far from the ideal, romanticized illusions that some couples imagine when they decide to start a family.

Most parents adjust, making the transition from ideal fantasy to practical reality, but those who do not may become rejecting or actually violent in their disillusion.

Full of organic expectation of nurture and love, the newborn opens itself into this world and meets with coldness. This coldness may be consistent or periodic. It may be at the level of resentment and hostility or, tragically, it may be full-blown hate. At whatever intensity or constancy it occurs, a deep conclusion that 'I am not safe' wires into the unconscious mind engendering the core of the Magical personality which is fright, even terror.

This Magical piece might be only a thread within the fabric of the overall personality or it may be a dominant aspect in the weave of character. To whatever extent it is present, this 'Magical factor' will have a distinct effect on how the person feels about themselves, others and the world generally. A Magical component, however small, in someone you work for or with or wish to influence requires particular attention if you are to access their quite wonderful gifts of loyalty, creativity and integrity.

Because this wound occurs during the first six months of life, the 'fright circuit' it engenders lies deep within the unconscious mind, from whence it may be triggered by events in current daily life. At the end of this section there are detailed suggestions as to how to manage someone with a Magical factor in their personality. Most important is an understanding of how deep and pervasive this fear circuit goes and why.

Coldness is the greatest threat to human life. In catastrophic tragedies like earthquakes, floods or wars, the first and most crucial call for help is always the same. It is not water or food that is the first urgency. The primary need is for blankets and tents. If the people do not get shelter from the cold, they die. This metaphor of the impact of physical coldness on exposed human beings reflects the effect of psychic coldness on the life of a newborn. When a cold threat is the response an infant meets on entering the world of others, s/he feels unwelcome and therefore terrified. Alexander Lowen called this dreadful state 'fear of annihilation'.[6]

Although actual rejection is the worst case, it is not the only instance that can lead to this debilitating conclusion. Jean Liedloff's breathtakingly painful account of normal babyhood in our culture in the last century is a stunning evocation of both the vulnerability of the human infant and our culture's one-time insensitivity to what ought to be common sense.

'Historically, in the maternity wards of the Western world there has been little chance of consolation. The newborn infant, with his skin crying out for smooth, warmth-radiating, skin-to-skin touch was, often still is, wrapped in dark lifeless cloth and put in a box where he is left, in motionless limbo – for the first time in all his body's experience – no matter how he cries. The only sounds he can hear are the wails of other victims of the same agonizing state. The sound can mean nothing to him. He cries and cries, his lungs new to air, are strained with the desperation in his heart. No one comes. Trusting in the rightness of life, as by nature he must, he does the only act he can, which is to cry on. Eventually, a timeless lifetime later, he falls asleep exhausted.'[7]

If a baby has a long stay in such a place, perhaps due to its being premature or to illness, similar negative conclusions about being wanted and welcome may be drawn. The actuality of love is masked and lost in an assumed reality based upon the sensations of the moment, which register directly on the nascent body-mind.

One of my Magical clients – who came from a very loving family – suffered from an allergy to her mother's milk. The nurture of her caregiver literally threatened her life. Eventually, doctors discovered what was causing the agonizing pain that this little baby was suffering, but not before these experiences left a mark within her body-mind form.

In instances such as these the Magical thread is not so deeply established within the personality because subsequent loving experiences mend and mediate the wounds. Nevertheless, the scars are there. In the truly unwelcoming home, the wounds of babyhood are reopened on a regular basis.

The negative characteristics will be far more extensive when the coldness is constant than when it is a moment in time or experienced only periodically. Out of this threatening and painful crucible comes the Magical personality with its developmental issues and with its exquisite gifts.

Parents are the most important formative factor in the development of personality but they are not always the cause of the wounds that determine personality form. A traumatic birth or – as indicated above – a babyhood illness in the most loving environment will leave a Magical scar if it registers in the body-mind as a threat to existence.

Such is the case of Angela, the much-loved daughter of my dear friend and colleague Sarah. I playfully refer to Sarah as 'my Demeter chum'. Demeter, you will remember, is the Earth Mother in Greek mythology who literally moved 'heaven and earth' to retrieve her daughter Persephone from her kidnap by Hades, god of the underworld. I think you will sense why Sarah has this place in my imagination when I tell you the story of what happened following Angela's premature birth decades ago, when a harsh and mechanistic science set the culture in most hospitals.

Angela was born two months prematurely. This was a very serious matter in the late 1970s. Of course she was immediately placed in an incubator to sustain her delicate life. In those days there was little or no understanding of the sustaining power of the mother-baby bond. At least that was the case in the hospital where Angela was born. Nowadays, mothers and fathers are encouraged to be present with their tiny premature infant and, through large sterile gloves built into the incubator, hold their baby sending their love and care through their touch. Can it possibly be a surprise that survival rates of premature babies increase when they can feel the powerful and loving presence of their parents?

In the hospital where Sarah gave birth to Angela, the cultural attitude seemed to be that parents were something of a nuisance. 'Get out of our way and let us save this baby' was the feeling Sarah experienced as she desperately sought to be near Angela in the incubator ward. It is typical now for parents to visit their incubated babies whenever they want and to stay for as long as they can. In 1978 Sarah was allowed to be near Angela only during strict visiting hours. For a week Sarah sat in the waiting room streaming with hormonal tears desperately waiting until she was allowed access to Angela.

I know the potency of my friend's emotions and – in the face of this gross insensitivity on the part of staff – I can imagine that she was a force to be reckoned with. Eventually, she was denied access to the waiting room and forbidden to be in the hospital building except during visiting hours. Terrible.

Baby Angela, for her part, protested her mother's absence with such righteous outrage that the nurses named her 'the voice'. I would like to think that this was in affectionate recognition of Angela's demanding her organic rights to intimacy with her mother. But I am not sure. The anti-emotional and over-rational definition of care and healing in the mid to late 20th century was often frighteningly mechanistic.

Angela came home after two months in the hospital to an ideal environment of orbiting warmth and care. Moreover, her life throughout the rest of her formative years was more than 'good enough'. As a result, her physical form today is strong, symmetrical and robust with an athletic appearance revealing a preponderance of the Hero Huntress form within her personality.

However, Angela's eyes – which are remarkably beautiful – have a blazing brightness that belies the 'startle' wiring of her fearful experiences in babyhood. As a combination of 'Sprite and Huntress', Angela is more on edge and wary than a pure Huntress Hero type. Her reaction to sudden pressure and challenge is to 'pull back' rather than 'step in' as is typical of the Hero. When under pressure, the look in Angela's eyes changes to the other manifestation of the Magical: 'eyeblock'. Her gaze becomes inaccessible and far away, melting into a 'spaced out' look that makes little or no contact. This process of 'dissociation' is a deeper and more debilitating response to pressure than the startle. The latter is connected to the 'fight/flight' mobilizing response in the brain stem and it indicates and initiates 'life preserving' action. Dissociation, on the other hand, manifests a deeper 'freeze/faint' aspect where an organism gives up on life and capitulates. Angela's tendency to startle and dissociate when under pressure is the legacy of that fright of her earliest months of life and represents the Magical thread in the overall garment of her personality. Nevertheless, what she lacks in boldness, she makes up for in imagination. Angela works in marketing and a big part of her success is her capacity for creative and lateral (non-rational) thinking, which pleases her clients and delights her boss.[8]

When Magical is an aspect of a personality form rather than the major component, the body will be stronger than the slight, tight and angular form that is classic for the type. It is in the eyes that the presence of the Magical element will always be seen. Each of the five Centaur types has a distinctive look in their eyes. Two types (the Magical Wizard/Sprite and the Superhero Superman/Wonder Woman) have eye tension, albeit of very different sorts. It is important to recognize eye tension and to know that it invariably indicates the possibility of some degree of paranoia. Individuals with eye tension when under pressure do not see reality. *They see what they fear.* That is the nature of paranoia.

Early fright can cause a retreat from bonding with a mother figure. This is something like a 'refusal to enter' the world of others, which leads to a failure to connect to the sensual world. As a result, development of the all-important 'reality function' is compromised.

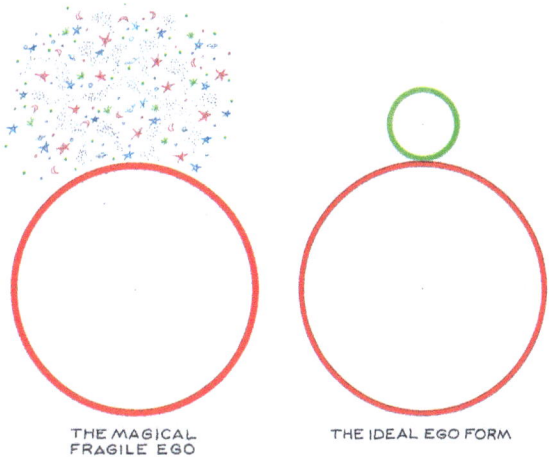

THE MAGICAL FRAGILE EGO

THE IDEAL EGO FORM

The downside of this 'refusal to enter' is illustrated in the image of the 'ego form' of the Magical when compared with the ideal. The shattering effect of fright scatters the energetic potential that would in better circumstances begin forming the ego. The pressure or the 'frustration' of the world is too much and damage is done.

On the other hand, this refusal to enter the world means that a part of the Magical remains out 'among the stars'. Below is an image meant to capture the thinking style of the Magical. Again, there is a shattered and scattered aspect to it that reflects the disorganizing impact of fright. Indeed, Magical thinking can be a bit 'all over the place'. Yet, this manner of thinking is wide-ranging – multi-perspectival we might say – with a capacity to link diverse aspects, thoughts and perceptions. This is a good definition for creativity, and the ability to come up with innovative and groundbreaking ideas and solutions is characteristic of the Magical personality type.

MAGICAL MULTI-PERSPECTIVAL THINKING

Although very far from the ideal, both the ego image and the thinking-pattern diagrams capture the nature of creative thinking with its lateral scope and multiple perspectives. Magicals characteristically see things from many different – often remarkable – viewpoints. It is not surprising that a number of our greatest scientists have a sizeable thread of Magical in their personality make-up.

The Magical Wizard/Sprite body form reflects their journey into the world. The infant's first response to a perceived cold and threatening environment is fright. This is closely followed by rage. It is a poignant and encouraging insight into our human spirit that even in this helpless state we spontaneously mobilize to fight for our rights. However, the overwhelming message the infant receives within this formative crucible – whether actual or assumed – is the denial of a right to exist. Terror and the rage are huge passions that are too big for such a little body to contain and express. They are shattering to both physical and mental systems.

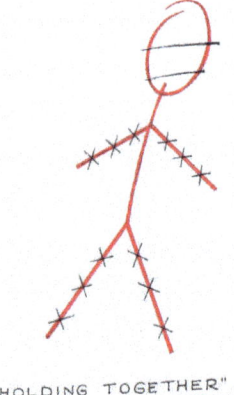

"HOLDING TOGETHER" AGAINST THE SHATTERING IMPACT OF FRIGHT

An energetic pattern of deep tension holds the organism together against this shattering as every joint in the body tightens to *hold* body and mind *together*. 'My feelings threaten my life' is an assumption that has a real base in this history.

With tragic expediency the infant turns against her own feelings and controls them by deadening her body. To stop the flow of these dangerous sensations and passions the child holds her breath, sucking in her belly and stiffening her musculature into tight, deep contractions. In this way the

Magical Wizard/Sprite *holds together* against inner as well as outer threats, both of which are potentially shattering.

In doing this, the baby loses a sense of herself as a physical entity. As our bond with reality is through our senses, she loses her ground and becomes disembodied by spacing out, leaving a pain-filled body. In due course, the growing child supports this state with a mental stance of 'mind over matter': intellect and spirit will rule body and emotion.

The more the Wizard or Sprite splits off from their physical and emotional aspects, the more they lose contact with practical reality. This lack of concrete focus is a major difficulty for these personalities when they enter managerial grades. What's more, the lack of a feeling quality can make relaxed and easy communication with others difficult. It is this separation from the physical self that lies behind what Lowen called an 'as if' quality to the Magical style of relating. They act as if they feel, but the warmth and immediacy of genuine contact can be missing.

When individuals have stronger elements within their personality along with a Magical thread, the body will be fuller and rounded (if Guardian) or stronger and more muscled (if Hero). Look to the eyes to determine whether a Magical factor is present. Whether blazing and bright, locked in the startle response or far away and detached, Magical eyes indicate the formative fright that is central to this personality.

The Magical Worldview

On the basis of their assumed reality, the Magical Wizard/Sprite mind concludes:

- *I am fragile.*

- *Others can be a threat to me.*

- *The world is a dangerous place.*

The Magical Wizard/Sprite at Work

The Magical Wizard/Sprite personality makes for a valuable but rather complex and sometimes difficult individual at work. Their value is in their ability to 'think outside the box'. When managed well they can produce strikingly creative ideas and solutions. They do especially well in research and development where a capacity for creative thinking is valued. They also thrive when and where there is a need for a precise and exquisite technical excellence.

Magicals can become very deeply immersed in whatever they are doing and are often perfectionists. As a result, they frequently lose track of the necessities of the bottom line as they follow their ideas to imaginative extremes or seek for the perfect technical solution. This can cause less creative but more realistic types to get exasperated and cry 'airy fairy' or 'head in the clouds' as they demand to be given something to finish the task or sell to the customer.

Wizards and Sprites are committed and hardworking and because of this they get promoted and then the pain begins. In most companies the way up the hierarchy involves leaving technical expertise and moving toward managerial responsibilities. When it comes to dealing with people instead of ideas, this type enters their area of difficulty. They face their developmental issues: fear of contact and lack of assertion.

Deep inside, a Magical is afraid of contact with others. When the currency of their day changes from thinking about ideas to dealing with people, they can become distressed and even paranoid. When stressed in this way, their expressions and even their physical movements are often jerky and ill-timed. They may be seen as rude and uncaring. Actually they are frightened and unsure.

In their pure form the Magical Wizards/Sprites lack a confident and easy way of being in the world. Flexible assertion in the face of conflict is especially challenging. Often they will withdraw from difficult situations, while at other times they unexpectedly flip to an opposite extreme, taking a fixed and implacable stance that appears aggressive, even violent to others. Whatever is actually happening, the 'assumed reality' is a life-or-death scenario, which triggers the primitive fight/flight mechanism way down in the brain stem. This can result in inappropriate and sometimes extreme behaviour. When a Magical thread is a part of a more robust personality form such as Guardian or Hero, these interpersonal issues will be less extreme while the capacity for unusual solutions and creative thinking remains.

Pressure can bring out the best in many personalities but it is not good for Magicals. Sudden changes and emergencies or multiple responsibilities can be shattering. We saw an instance of this in Sam's response to intense and sudden pressure from Peter in our introductory case study.

Another Magical Wizard case study from our flagship leadership programme at Cranfield School of Management some years ago illustrates further Magical issues, including the fact that many of them do not wish to become leaders.

Keith came to our programme because, quite suddenly, he had to manage people – a lot of them – and he was not at all sure he was up to this new task. Keith was in the throes of a crisis that regularly faces individuals who are a success within the area of their technical expertise. They do so well that they get promoted. As they make their way up the organization, they move away from a technical base and towards the totally new arena of managerial responsibility.

Often such individuals are propelled into managerial responsibility without any acknowledgement that this new task is very different from the technical one they are leaving behind. Frequently they are given no training whatsoever to meet the challenges of dealing with people.

Keith was not that unlucky. He worked for a large scientific research company that uses the management school at Cranfield regularly. Keith was a research scientist – a brilliant one. He had done well in his career and he clearly loved research. From a Centaur perspective, Keith was primarily a Magical Wizard in character with very little of the stronger, more grounded elements (Guardian or Hero) in his personality structure.

On the first day of the programme he found his place in the front row of the lecture theatre and resolutely prepared to become a manager. Initially he was uneasy with the notion of psychology, but very quickly his bright and lateral mind opened to the excitement of exploring a new model of how things work. A crucial turning point occurred when he let go of the image of the human heart as a 'pump' and embraced the poetic notion of an organic centre for feeling and value. Being both bright and open, Keith quickly identified with the Magical Wizard pattern, with its qualities of creativity and integrity and its fear of contact. He found the description of the formative crucible of the Magical movingly consistent with what he knew (by report) of his own troubled babyhood. Moreover, he identified within himself the haunting insecurity and lack of self-confidence which is the poignant core of the Magical personality. Once validated, these feelings surfaced into consciousness in quite a powerful manner and Keith let himself be aware that he did not want to be responsible for eighty people.

The course tutors were also concerned about this rather huge management responsibility for such a fragile and non-assertive man. Keith loved ideas but he did not much care for people, especially *en masse*. Most especially he dreaded the idea of having to tell them what to do. Moreover, the prospect of having his door hypothetically open to eighty of them was tangibly painful for him. On the other hand, he was grateful for the acknowledgement of his value to the company represented by the promotion. Characteristically, he felt he had a choice only to 'take it' or 'leave it'. Magical Wizard/Sprites typically think in such black-and-white terms.

Within the supportive context of his small development group, Keith was encouraged by his tutor and fellow delegates to look afresh at his situation. Certainly he was valued by the organization and it was clear to everyone that he was exceptionally bright and remarkably creative.

He was asked to brainstorm about what managerial position might be a good fit for him. Keith visualized a small research team of smart, self-motivated specialists with whom he would be happy to work and where he could comfortably (well, at least not too *uncomfortably*) be 'first among equals' in a leadership role.

On the basis that the worst that could happen was that his boss would say 'no', Keith left with an action plan to discuss this possibility back at work. At best he would get the kind of managerial role he wanted. If the best did not happen, he would at least have opened a dialogue regarding the company's proposal of what was, for him, too big a step into leadership.

The end of the story is a happy one. Like many Magicals, Keith had little idea of how much he was valued by his company. The more enlightened of his superiors had themselves been concerned about his ability to take on the role offered. The extent of the responsibility had, in fact, been a reflection of how much they rated him and wanted him to stay within the organization. His boss was relieved at Keith's more realistic proposal and delighted to give him exactly what he wanted.

Keith returned to the second module of our programme very pleased at what he had secured for his career with his new insight into himself and with 'a little help from his friends'.

Gifts of the Magical

At their best, the Magical personality is characterized by:

Creativity – They often have a remarkable capacity to see things from an unusual perspective.

Depth – They seem to be profoundly aware of the value and meaning of life.

Integrity – They are rigorously honest. Falsehood can be almost impossible for them. I am sure that in another age, it was these people who stubbornly died at the stake for their beliefs.

The Magical Shadow

Withdrawn – They can be spaced out and disengaged.

Unrealistic – They tend toward perfectionism and can have difficulty with deadlines as a result. Their tendency to idealism may lead them to have negative judgements about colleagues who are committed to more commercial objectives.

Violent – Quite extreme outbursts may occur when they feel pushed over a tolerance limit which has not been made clear to others.

What the Magical Brings

There is a transcendent quality to these individuals, as if they have not totally become a part of this world. This notion helps in understanding the Wizard's gift. Magicals are never fully grounded in conventional reality and so their thinking is freer and more lateral.

All people have the capacity to be creative but it is highly developed in the Magical because it is used so often in order to escape the perceived dangers of the real world. In the physical body, any muscle that is used a lot becomes strong and highly developed. It is the same with mental potentials. Those which are engaged most often become strong characteristics within the personality. Creativity is a potential that the Magicals bring to any situation. A mindful manager knows how to provide the right atmosphere so that this potential can be accessed for the good of the task, the team and the organization.

Good managers and good friends are also mindful that Magicals may use this creative capacity in a defensive way that limits their participation in daily life.

Years ago as a participant in a personal development group, I was describing a nasty political situation at work. I was keen to (creatively) reposition events so that I would not have to confront the wrongdoing, which threatened to damage my career chances. A sour-faced but truth-telling group member growled, 'The trouble with you, Sandy, is when somebody pisses on you, you say it's raining.' He was right. I was misusing my imagination to avoid having to respond to the pressures of the world.

Integrity and depth are also characteristic qualities in the Magical Wizard/Sprite personality. Colleagues often appreciate their loyalty and honesty. Perhaps the early retreat from the perceived cold, scary world takes them back into their spiritual essence where a part of them remains. As with creativity, such easy access to the spiritual can be used inappropriately and defensively. I had a client who never confronted events in his life, believing that the 'laws of karma' would deliver punishment to wrongdoers in the end. Psychologists call this type of avoidance 'spiritualizing' and it needs handling in organizational life. Nevertheless, it is also true that Magicals tend to be less materially motivated than other types. The more this form is present within an individual personality the less they will desire to climb the material ladder of success, especially at the cost of personal ethics.

Limiting Attitudes of the Magical

When a baby is born expecting a warm welcome and feels not wanted, s/he concludes 'There is something deeply wrong with me.' In reality it is the environment and not the baby that is wrong here. However, a newborn cannot discriminate between self and other or self and world. As a result, the sense of wrongness becomes a primary experience of self: *I feel bad therefore I am bad.* Nothing could be further from the truth, but this assumed reality is established in that implicit layer of memory and can remain unchallenged and unconscious throughout life, rendering the individual unconfident and unsure. Later, when the child's mind has evolved the capacity to discriminate, there is a poignant sense to the lack of re-evaluation that is typical. After all, which is a more frightening thought for a child of any age:

'There is something wrong with me.'

or

'There is something wrong with those who are supposed to be taking care of me.'

So, even after the capacity for reflective thought is established, the earlier misconception is maintained as an unconscious defence against fright and neglect. Another version of the same principle causes abused children to defend and protect violent and/or neglecting parents. Moreover, this misconception – that 'there is something wrong with me' – provides some modicum of control in an overwhelming situation. 'If the problem is *me*, then *maybe I can fix me*. If I can get me right, then maybe I'll be loved or safe or valued.'

This is the germ of the perfectionism that characterizes much Magical behaviour at work. 'If I can get it perfect, I am safe' is a deep-seated attitude that acts as a defence against unconscious fright. This kind of magical thinking where we 'make deals' with life is a characteristic of childhood and the threads of it reside in all of us. The way Magicals cling to perfection plays a big part in many of their lives. It can cause real difficulty at work, especially in times when organizations are scaling down and everyone has to take on more responsibility. Sometimes there is simply not time for perfection. However, when being perfect is unconsciously equated with safety in a dangerous world, it can be difficult or even impossible to relinquish.

In the adult world of organizational life these attitudes produce a characteristic mode that is less than effective. Attuned understanding and mindful management can move these creative but ill-at-ease individuals into more grounded and connected ways of being with others and themselves at work. These will be articulated shortly in the section entitled 'Mindful Management'.

Personal Development for the Magical Wizard/Sprite

Mind Work: A new idea about self-value

There is a deeply unconscious attitude of mind that seems to 'haunt' the Magical personality. In a classroom exercise I group the personality types into 'tribes' so they can teach each other about the differences between their worldviews. Because my programmes are for managers, it is rare to have a 'pure' Magical on a course and so individuals with a sizeable piece of Wizard or Sprite in their makeup sit together to represent this type.

Whatever threads of the stronger ego forms are present within their personalities, this group always resonates with sad and affirming nods when I suggest that Magicals harbour a deep conviction that 'there is something deeply wrong with me' and 'when people really know me they will not rate me'.

Of course most of us have thoughts like this from time to time, but such self-negating beliefs go much deeper in Magicals and they have a debilitating effect on their self-confidence and ease in life. Sitting together with a group of others who harbour this same wounding attitude, Magicals open up and talk about how this grave self-doubt undermines their performance at work and their pleasure in life. This process is healing and – like ghosts in the sunlight – the haunting self-doubts begin to evaporate as they are understood and shared. Such sharing is also helpful to other more naturally confident types who can then transfer this awareness to interactions with Magicals back at work. In my experience, active insight into the inner struggles of others changes behaviour far more than lectures and seminars on the differences in personality.

To help with a change of mind, I invite the Magicals to remember that according to Centaur theory they would have suffered a perceived 'miss' of some kind in babyhood when 'psychology and physiology are one'. Any misadventure for an infant feels bad and because psychological identity and physical state are not yet differentiated, the baby 'mind' deduces 'I feel bad, therefore, I am bad'. It is touching to recall the dawning relief on the faces of many of these Magical students as they consider the possibility that a disturbing inner certainty may be the result of a *misperception* of their nature and value in their earliest months of life. They were and are essentially good. Something in their environment was *not good for them* and because of that they got a wrong idea about themselves. Often this consideration leads to some philosophical musing, which Magicals do rather well. New and more positive thoughts about their true nature and their potential are free to emerge.

Body Work: Two types of body work are recommended:

1. Anything that warms, relaxes and opens the locked joints helps release the deep pattern of fear from the body. Hot baths, massage or gentle stretching movements as in yoga and t'ai chi all work to this end.

2. A commitment to building fitness, both in areas of stamina and strength, helps erase the attitude of being a helpless creature in a dangerous world. Remember, the mind and the body dynamically interact. When the body is strong and vibrant the mind will automatically shift toward a more life-affirming direction.

Any acknowledging and working through of blocked feelings will awaken the deep potential within. With focus and commitment misconceived attitudes about personal value and the world can be shifted toward the positive. This can, in time, enable a fuller and more vibrant expression of self.

The Mindful Management of the Magical Wizard/Sprite

A simple something that makes them relax: ACCEPTANCE

Protect these individuals from pressure and sudden surprises. They do not like short-term challenge or long-term responsibility, and they need a safe space to do their creative thing. The more Guardian or Hero strands within the personality, the less this will be the case.

Don't back them into a corner. Respect their need for space and time. When the heat is on and the bottom line calls, more practical types can become frustrated with the Magical's failure to respond to deadlines. Remember, the more you pressure them, the more they withdraw. Furthermore, if you push them into what they feel to be an entrapped situation, they can explode in a violent manner.

Softly, softly is the best approach. (Warning: the soft approach will not be rated by Guardians and Heroes who will read it as patronizing.)

Provide a warm and supportive atmosphere. Remember, the original wound was a perceived cold threat to their being in the world. Affirm what you value in them on a regular basis. This must be what you really think and feel. Magicals quickly see through insincerity. When you rate them make sure to tell them, and not just once – often.

When correction is necessary, begin with reassurance of their value, remember they can quickly go into a 'life or death' wiring unconsciously. Then be careful to criticize the behaviour not the person and be sure to do this privately. Follow any discipline with warmth.

Monitor reality with them and keep in touch. Creativity can take them down unrealistic tracks and keep in mind that they are motivated by innovative ideas rather than the completion of a task. Magicals can get lost in their thinking and miss deadlines. The more realistic and grounded (Guardian and Hero) threads there are in the fabric of their personality, the less this will be the case.

Help them manage their creativity (for example: 'Let's jot that down and come back to it later'). They can be scatty and good ideas can be lost.

Link them into communications systems as they easily make paranoid assumptions. When they feel disliked or threatened they withdraw in fear rather than test reality. You will need to seek them out and help them see the simple truth of what is going on. It is as if the eye tension blocks and distorts their view of reality. Under pressure they see what they fear rather than what is actually happening.

The assessment and scrutiny inevitably involved in promotion scenarios will cause them to contract and therefore they may not present themselves well. They find such situations very painful. Use your sensitivity and kindness to help them through such unavoidable processes.

In summary, the mindfully managed Magical Wizard or Sprite can be a source of creativity, commitment, honesty and loyalty. They are rather high-maintenance but when they are well-managed they are very often worth the effort.

Handling the Magical Wizard/Sprite Client

Do not frighten them. Because this type is above the reality line, adequate, healthy relating can be seen as 'too much'. Heroes need to realize that the healthy presence of their robust ego energy can be perceived as a threat and even as bullying (which Heroes *never* intend).

Approach slowly and subtly. Keep your voice and your energy quiet and calm.

Do not rush, push or crowd. Give them time and space, *which they read as respect*, and they will give you the business again and again. Once they decide to trust you, they remain very loyal to you.

Following on from the above, it is wise to expect *not* to close the deal immediately. Be willing to leave it with them so they can relax, think and decide they are safe with you. Note: such a sales approach to a Hero would be seen as uncommitted and questionable and – worst of all – a waste of their time.

True Magicals are very private, so unless they have a thread of a more social type, they will not be comfortable with any discussion that is non-technical or outside work. By all means suggest lunch or dinner if that is etiquette but be aware they may well not want to go. Be ready to let them off that social hook.

Magicals are prone to paranoia, so it is important to be very clear and very careful lest you are misunderstood. If you feel this is happening, take the time and make the effort to clarify issues after you have stepped back and given them space.

Behave honourably. These people have a lot of integrity. They value relationships of trust and typically their word is their bond.

THE ROMANTICS: The Poet and the Damsel

This personality form is created around the Right to Nourishment, which is formative during the first year of life.

Once established in existence, the baby needs to be fed. In psychological development this refers more to emotional and energetic stimulation rather than to food. Babies need to be cuddled, talked to, fussed over and given the attention and attending they demand. I would add 'within reason' but the notion of what is reasonable is subjective. This opens the door to those who maintain that parents need to 'show the baby who is boss'. During babyhood the power differential is awesomely on the side of the big people and any glory in winning a battle of wills against someone who can't even turn over by themselves is inappropriate and has heartbreaking repercussions.

Babies are meant to be babied. Babyhood is the one time in our lives when another person can and should meet all of our needs. If a baby ever truly experiences the extent of its helplessness, the parenting has not been 'good enough'. To some degree, he or she will not move fully into the next stage of development and insofar as the need of that stage is not met, a scar will form within the body-mind. As we will discover the scars left by lack of welcome and warmth differ from those caused by deprivation of nourishment. However, what is common to both is what can be called an 'organic lack of confidence'. Individuals wounded in either of the first two stages that comprise babyhood are less robust, less sure of themselves and less able to handle the world than those whose babyhood was generous or at least adequate.

The Developmental Crucible of the Romantic Poet/Damsel

The second (Romantic) formative crucible occurs marginally later in babyhood than that of the Magical personality.

In a hypothetically pure case of this type there is good enough environmental support for the baby to conclude it is welcome and in this second babyhood-based personality there is not the deep fright that marks the Magical form.

As a result, personal value is to some extent anchored and the world and those that live in it are not seen as threatening. Nevertheless, the baby's birthright of a maintained sense of ease and security is not optimally met. The Romantic wound is not caused by a perceived sense of cold threat of some kind, but by *the emptiness of a non-responsive environment.* Nobody threatens the baby's life but others do not respond enough and the world is melancholy as a result.

As always, the innate temperament of the infant plays a part. This genetic component is always a feature in the formation of a way-of-being in the world. For example, an infant with an introverted temperament will want less attention and may not be affected by parents who are less engaged. Or an extrovert baby, whose hard-wiring requires more stimulation, will likely protest more vividly when parents are less involved. In an optimal scenario, these less active parents will 'wake up and hear the baby'. Ideally, parents are affected and instructed by their babies. For the most part, I am sure this is true of the parents who come to my programmes. The 'worrying' that I sense from them when I begin to teach about the formative years bodes well for their babies.

However, whether introvert or extrovert, all babies need a lot of attention. That some infants temperamentally require less is true, but it is a small truth compared to the big truth that parenting an infant well is very hard work. If caregivers do not take up this tough task and provide an attentive and stimulating context, the baby does not thrive and the impact is both mental, in terms of unhelpful life attitudes, and physical in terms of a compromised energy level that remains an issue throughout their life.

A simple way of understanding the connection between experience in babyhood and energy level is to imagine that a human infant is born with a fully formed but uncharged 'battery'. The energetic system is in place but it must be charged and this must happen during the first year of life. This gives an interesting perspective on all of the 'coo-cooing' and fussing we do with infants to entertain them and to gain for ourselves that heavenly baby smile.

Parents and others stimulate and charge the energetic system of the infant through eye contact, facial expressions and baby games like peek-a-boo. Psychologists now believe that the attention babies demand is vital to their psychological and physical development during this first year of life. Perhaps this is why infants demand attention so fiercely when they do not get it. At least, they do until the pain of disappointment in a non-responsive environment causes them to fall into the silence of despair.

Sadly, this silence is often perceived by grown-ups as the baby having 'learned who is boss'. This is not the case. The baby's brain has not yet achieved the maturity to understand a concept like 'boss'. That capacity is years away. What the baby does learn is a lesson about the validity of *effort*. A negative conclusion is drawn, one that will cause considerable difficulty for the individual later in life, most especially around an attitude to work.

The image here denotes the thinking pattern of the Romantic Damsel/Poet and it reflects the sense of 'energy gaps' or a more pervasive lack of stamina. Romantic Damsels/Poets typically exhibit an erratic and fluctuating engagement and commitment. This is particularly true if a personality contains a large component of this form. Characteristically, they thrive when another person is focused on them and giving them attention. Then they often come up with bright ideas and contribute excited comments. However, for reasons to be described below, motivation is not anchored inside and so when left on their own, they flag and falter. Strategies for how to deal with and develop this 'energy issue' typical of the Romantic Damsel/Poet are listed under the Mindful Management heading at the end of this section.

Returning to the crucible that creates the Romantic Damsel/Poet, the core issue is lack of attention and social stimulation. The worst clinical picture shows parents who are unable to be a reliable and adequate resource for the baby's emotional needs. Extreme cases reveal histories of parental alcoholism, psychological depression or serious physical illness. In more ordinary examples, parents may be too busy with work or other responsibilities to give the baby all the attention that is necessary for full development. In any number of scenarios, too little stimulation and attention occurs, resulting in a personality form that tends to be over-dependent and lacking in energy and vitality.

As with the origin of the Magical personality, the causative scenario need not be as extreme as in depression or disease in the caregiver. Another frequent cause of the Romantic personality occurs in families where the adults are fit and happy and eager to be good parents. They have just read the wrong books. A whole generation of mothers raised their babies on a rigid four-hour feeding schedule. In such cases, optimal parenting *can* occur when the infant happens to have a 'four-hour system', however damage is done when the baby's time clock does not match the textbook. Whatever the cause, there appears to be a direct link between a non-responsive environment during babyhood and a dysfunctional work ethic in adult life characterized by lack of commitment to a task in hand, which is sometimes perceived as laziness.

Let's look at it from a narrative perspective. From the moment of birth, a baby must 'work' to get the resources it needs to achieve the organic 'task' of developing and growing. These resources are physical and emotional attention and stimulation. A baby gets these supplies by signalling a need to the environment through crying – and so the *work* a baby does to achieve their *task* (growth) is to cry. An infant literally sings for his or her supper. If we place this energetic understanding alongside a 'show-the-baby-who-is-boss' scenario we gain insight into a key aspect of the Romantic personality.

Imagine a household where parents are dedicated to the classic four-hour schedule and that unbeknownst to them, their baby has a two-and-a-half-hour system. After the morning feed the child is put at the bottom of the garden in the (cold) fresh air to sleep (alone) until its next feed. After two and a half hours the baby awakes hungry. 'Right,' s/he muses, 'time to go to work and get the supplies I need to achieve my task of growing and developing.' The infant's mother hears the cries, checks her watch and reminds herself that it is good to let a baby cry because crying (alone and cold) will strengthen the lungs. Meanwhile, the baby is furiously *working away* and getting no response. S/he gets tired eventually and falls asleep but hunger hurts and so s/he does not sleep for long. Awaking, s/he goes to work again. The pattern goes on eternally because for a baby there is no such thing as the future, only the here and now.

The infant is faced with a brutal reality of *effort followed by no response*. As this experience continues, the baby inadvertently concludes that effort is useless – 'so why bother?' A 'why bother, it won't work out anyway' attitude forms the unwholesome core of the Romantic Damsel/Poet work ethic. Deeper down in the unconscious mind is a sense of abandonment that is the source of the core feeling of the Romantic, which is deep sadness, even despair.

A large piece of the 'lazy bone' in this personality type comes from the low energetic charge explained earlier, but it is exacerbated by this central conviction based on lived experiences that effort leads nowhere. Such endemic cynicism is hard to change because it has grown out of actual experience within the formative crucible of this life phase.

Because necessary supplies do not arrive from the non-responsive environment, important aspects of development do not occur. There is a way in which the Romantic Poet/Damsel stays stuck (Freud would have said 'fixated') in babyhood. A 'babyish' tendency toward dependence is another key difficulty that managers have with the Romantic personality.

As mentioned previously, babyhood is a time when somebody else can and actually should meet all of our needs for us. Indeed, we all would agree that the world *does* owe a baby creature a living and that the big ones should look out for the little ones. Imagine that this right is imprinted on human consciousness from birth and the associated needs are like open vessels within the baby's psyche waiting to be filled. If parenting is good, the vessel of need is filled. What happens at that point can be compared to what occurs when we need a glass of water and somebody fills it. When our water glass is full, we don't want any more. If the water keeps coming we say, 'That's enough, thank you.' Babies are the same. Coming out of a generous babyhood they get to a point where they do not *want* the big ones to feed them, dress them, hold their hand and so on.

Unfortunately, as parents will undoubtedly know, this occurs before spoon coordination, awareness of left and right shoes and street wisdom are totally in place – but that is beside this particular point. What is clear is that with good enough parenting, the child stops identifying with that original right to be nurtured and totally cared for and moves resolutely toward independence. However, if the original vessel does not get filled, the unconscious mind does *not* relinquish those babyhood demands. In these individuals the archaic and unresolved convictions haunt the adult life through largely unconscious attitudes like 'the big people should be taking care of me'. If you are the manager of such an individual, guess who the big person is?

In conclusion, the wound of the Romantic Damsel/Poet is deprivation of emotional attention and stimulation. Whichever way this happens the resultant personality will have a specific quality. As always, the depth of this patterning depends on the extremity of the formative situation. A character-style Damsel or Poet will likely have a mix of another stronger personality threads within the fabric of their form (Hero is frequently found in such a mix) which will ameliorate the low-energy issue. As is the case in all five personality types, those further along Stephen Johnson's quantitative dimension (character style – neurotic – character disorder) will show more of the negative aspects and these will be more entrenched.

A poignant story from a course delegate will illustrate how a Romantic wound can arise out of a situation where all intentions are good. Small personal development groups are a feature of Centaur programmes. In these groups individuals typically share current concerns at work and also any awareness that has arisen in their minds regarding their childhood having heard the Centaur material. This particular delegate could hardly wait to share a new perspective coming out of his learning. 'I *know* my parents love me,' he confided, 'but I have never *felt* that they love me.' Perhaps you spot the operation of the left versus the right brain in his statement. You would be right. Here is his story. Joe is not his name, but we will call him Joe to make the story more accessible.

Joe was the only child of a hard-working country couple who ran a village grocery shop along with a van that travelled the environs of the village selling bread and other produce. With the birth of their son the couple resolved that they would dedicate their working lives to securing him an excellent private education. They did exactly that at considerable cost to their own comfort and pleasure. Joe had attended a modest private school and had achieved a first at a very good university. As Joe recounted his story, sharing with us details that his parents had told him about his past, a sad unfolding of a classic Romantic scenario impressed and touched us all.

Joe's mother was in charge of the shop, which was open seven days a week. His father drove the van and also did odd jobs for elderly citizens in the village, which meant he had full and busy days. His mother was equally busy in the shop and she often remarked to Joe that he had been a 'very cooperative' and 'good' baby who amused himself and slept a lot, which meant that she did not have to spend much time away from the shop attending to him. Joe most certainly was loved by these self-sacrificing parents, but the *baby* who was Joe in the first year of his life did not experience the stimulation, attention and energetic input that registers in the implicit memory system as being the joyously 'beloved one'.

The framing of his story within the Centaur context helped Joe understand the strange paradox of feelings that had perplexed him for years. Moreover, the poignancy of unintended consequences emerging from the good intentions of his parents served to increase his love for them even as he made plans to heal the wounds caused by his history. In line with Centaur recommendations, Joe committed to increasing his physical exercise before returning to module two of the programme in two months. He sheepishly admitted that he had suspected that exercise was good for him. He knew that he felt much better when he went jogging regularly, but he had never really wanted to admit this to himself because he often preferred the couch and TV to the running path. When Joe returned to module two at the end of the summer he was fit and brown and vibrant. He had also visited his parents where he had been able to thank them for their sacrifice without the inner ambivalence he had always felt before. As it happens, I work regularly in the organization where Joe is now a senior manager. I see him often and he continues to thrive.

The impact of lack of stimulation and attention is clear in the image of the Romantic ego form when viewed in comparison with the ideal. Although a discernible shape is clear (especially when compared to the scattered ego of the Magical Wizard/Sprite) the form lacks strength. It is as if the lack of parental input is reflected in the weakness of the line delineating the ego. One can imagine that under pressure this form would collapse.

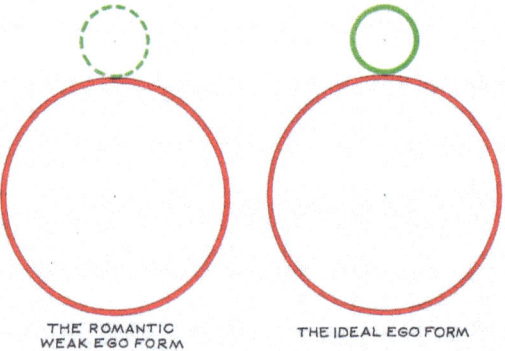

THE ROMANTIC WEAK EGO FORM   THE IDEAL EGO FORM

As was the case with the ego form of the Magical Wizard/Sprite, this image also illustrates one of the gifts of the Romantic personality. The ego is permeable and so the deeper aspects of Romantic Damsel/Poet are more accessible. The actual weakness of their ego results in Romantics being more reachable in a way that the Hero type – with their robust and strong ego – are not. I find it touching that the wounds that give us our 'developmental issue' are typically the source of our unique gifts.

There is little tension in the pure Damsel or Poet body. It is only in the throat – where the expression of need has been stifled – that this tension is apparent.

Remember, tension is the result of blocked energy and the chronic difficulty of this personality is low energy and therefore their bodies typically are over-relaxed. In pure types, the posture is stooped. The shoulders slope. The chest caves in and the pelvis slouches forward. The stance overall has a collapsed appearance.

The Romantic Damsel/Poet often seems younger than their age. They have an easy-going, languid look. A characteristic elongation of form gives them an elegant and graceful appearance. Arms and legs are long, slim or even lanky. The face is typically a long oval and the torso is narrow for its length.

"HOLDING ON" TO AVOID A SENSE OF ABANDONMENT

Lowen suggests that because the musculature is undercharged due to lack of developmental stimulation, it does not contain the growth of the long bones, leaving them to overgrow. Whether or not this idea is scientifically sound, it evokes an understanding of an observed truth.[2]

The flow of aggression within a human body literally forms the jaw. Learning to 'read' the shape of a jaw gives one an immediate gauge of how available the 'fight' is in another. Aggression is energy and the Damsel/Poet lacks energy and therefore their aggressive function is underdeveloped. It follows that the jaw is soft, pointed rather than square, and even falls backward. The cruel caricature of the weedy, chinless wonder would have to be this personality.

Typically, Romantics have beautiful eyes that are relaxed and appealing. They can have a doe or spaniel quality. Unlike the over tense or unavailable eyes of the Magical, Romantic eyes seek and welcome contact.

The Romantic Worldview

On the basis of a perceived reality the Romantic Damsel/Poet mind completes their worldview statement and concludes:

- *I am in need.*
- *Others should take care of me.*
- *The world owes me a living.*

The Romantic at Work

The Romantic Poet/Damsel is a total contrast to the Magical Wizard/Sprite when it comes to relaxation. Magicals have far too much tension in their mind and body systems whereas Poets and Damsels appear to have too little. They are also opposites in interpersonal style. Magicals avoid contact. Romantics seek it out.

On seeing a Damsel or Poet colleague approaching down a hallway, many people increase their walking speed or take a detour – anything to avoid being trapped into what is inevitably a lengthy conversation. Once started, a conversation with a Romantic Damsel/Poet can go on and on and, however committed we are to honesty, we can find ourselves telling outrageous lies in order to get away. 'I have to get back to my office because I am expecting a call from the Kremlin' or 'I need to take the dog to the vet because she is expecting kittens!'

Anything to be free from those appealing eyes that keep us entranced and those endless words, lulling us into motionless and compliant attendance. When we finally do get away we find ourselves drained of energy. At such a moment we have experienced the developmental issue of the Romantic Damsel/Poet style. This personality type has a chronically low energy resource. Figuratively, they have a flat battery and they go about with little energetic jump leads which they snap on to other people. Once hooked up, they charge up their energy battery from the focus and attention they get from their host. Sometimes this process is enacted under the guise of giving the other some necessary information but it often takes *forever*. If you rush or try to break off early with a Romantic type, they will be truly hurt and may take offence.

A live example of this within a team-building workshop for a well-known research and development lab occurred some years ago when I was working with my friend and colleague Jacey. Jacey is a perfect example of the very best of a Romantic/Hero combination. She is dynamic, rational and fair-minded and she is also open and social with a charming sense of humour. Here is how she used her personality to help educate a Romantic to the strain he was inflicting on his teammates with his (unconscious) need for attention.

Roger (our Romantic) was a renowned and remarkable expert in his area of expertise, and many of his colleagues had frequent need of his input to achieve their tasks and complete their projects. Their complaint was that once asked about some matter or another Roger would launch into a kind of dissertation on the subject when all they needed was a short, discrete answer to a specific point. As you might expect, this product research team was made up of commercial scientists. Many had large pieces of Hero in their personality form and so wanted to 'get on with the task' rather than hear about the back story of the issue in question.

When confronted with their feedback, Roger became defensive. 'What's wrong with me giving you that additional data? Those are valid facts. It is all perfectly good information.' After about three attempts at verbal feedback from the team, Jacey got to her feet, picked up a plate of bite-sized biscuits and popped one into Roger's mouth. It was about eleven in the morning, so a bite of biscuit would have been welcomed by us all. Moreover, Jacey is a pretty, charming woman and so for two reasons a surprised Roger accepted the biscuit with a smile and a 'thank you'. He swallowed the yummy morsel then and resumed his argument. At this point Jacey slipped another bite-sized biscuit into his mouth. Three times more as he began to talk, Jacey popped a biscuit into Roger's mouth.

At last he put up his hand saying, 'I don't want any more biscuits, thank you.'

Jacey replied, 'Why not? What's wrong with me giving you a biscuit at coffee time. These are all good biscuits I have here. Why shouldn't I give them to you?'

It only took a moment for this bright, good-humoured man to see the comparison with his force-feeding his teammates with unwanted information. His colleagues were affectionately delighted at the result of Jacey's clever metaphor. A realization that could not register verbally landed vividly and memorably when translated into a physical enactment.

Jacey and I worked with this team throughout the course of a year, during which the spirit of the team soared. After Jacey's creative intervention, Roger 'over-informed' his colleagues far less. When he did slip back to his old ways (as we all do from time to time) his teammate would place an affectionate hand on his shoulder and say, 'Would you like a biscuit, Rog?' This would both call up the new learning and recall the good will of the training workshop dedicated to protecting the spirit of the team from feelings of frustration and resentment.

Another difference between the Magicals and the Romantics is in their interpersonal style. A Wizard or Sprite colleague will keep you engaged for as short a time as possible because contact makes them nervous and tense. A Romantic will set up camp in your office for the day if you let them.

To be sure there are wonderful elements within this personality. They are genuinely open and friendly. Their ease with people can be a great asset in a team of over-serious types. With a practical joke or a box of cream cakes, the Romantics can crack tension and get everyone to take a breath or a break and get back to work refreshed.

What's more, because they love attention they often do wonderfully at presentations. Moreover, they network well because they love chatting with everyone and are relaxed in crowds. In fact, they fulfil any social aspect of their job gracefully and to good effect.

Like the Magicals, Romantic energy is centred in the head. Although their ideas are typically not as far out or creative as those of Magicals, they are usually bright and forthcoming. But be careful: Romantics tend to prefer thinking to doing and, in the worse cases, can be rather lazy about getting things finished. Their drive to get attention may cause them to come on strong at first in order to get noticed but they may lack the energy to stand their own ground or finish the task. Advice as to how to develop these delightful folk is listed under the mindful management reading at the end of the chapter.

When angry, Romantic Damsel/Poets may have difficulty in being straightforward. Truthful and forthright expression takes energy. Rather than coming out directly with a protest, they often lapse into complaining or, worse still, fall into silent resentment, which can lead to spiteful or undermining behaviour. For the same reason, any responsibilities which require sustained effort will be at risk. This apparent lack of commitment to the task drives colleagues who are dedicated to the bottom line absolutely mad.

When this easy-going, bright, relaxed Romantic thread is mixed with a stronger personality aspect – like the Hero – the energetic downsides disappear and leave an open, dynamic personality form which is frequently found in organizational life. This hybrid Romantic-Hero type is flexible and strong and such individuals make really good leaders. President Barack Obama is an excellent example of the Romantic-Hero combination where the predominance of the robust Hero aspect is softened and gentled by a small dash of Romantic Poet.

The Romantic Gifts

Sensitivity – They are genuinely open to the feelings of others.

Relaxation – Their laid-back ways bring a valuable element of pleasure and ease in organizational life.

Intelligence – They like thinking and come up with many bright ideas.

Playfulness – This quality contributes a fresh light-hearted atmosphere to the workplace and is good for team spirit.

The Romantic Shadow

Low Energy – They drain energy from others, usually by too much talking or over-explaining.

Lazy – They are unwilling or unable to follow things up or through.

Bitter – The quality of sweetness, which is so attractive in this personality type, can sour into cynicism or the verbal violence of sarcasm.

What the Romantic Brings

The Romantic Damsel/Poets often retain an openness, sensitivity and playfulness that is positive and delightfully childlike. These qualities are of considerable benefit in organizational life. There is no better tactic for the management of stress than a good laugh. The relaxed openness of the Romantic can be like fresh air in an over-tense work environment where focus on the task and nothing but the task reaches grim proportions.

Also, when a thread of Romantic is combined with a more robust form, the chronic difficulty of low energy is accordingly lessened and the positive aspects listed here remain. This produces a delightfully open and sensitive personality who is both dynamic and reliable. In these difficult days of constant change, the Poet Warrior or Damsel Huntress is proving to be a new and potent leadership form.

Limiting Attitudes of the Romantics

Because the classic Romantics have a genuinely low energy charge, things are harder for them than for other more robust types. The attitude that 'Life is unfair, particularly for me' is often found and given actual early deprivation there is some basis for this, but staying focused on self-sorrow will not help.

A related attitude that often infuriates colleagues is 'I am the only one who is really working hard.' This may arise from the misinterpretation of reality. Because of their low energy charge Romantics get tired more quickly than the energetic types.

Possibly the truth in what they are saying is 'I am the only one who is really tired.' It is then possible to draw a wrong conclusion that others are not working hard because they are not physically depleted. Other mistaken conclusions arising out of the Damsel/Poet early wiring include 'The world owes me a living' and 'Somebody big should be taking care of my life.' These attitudes can lead to the Romantic Damsel/Poet becoming quite a drain on managers and colleagues.

It is most difficult for goal-centred colleagues like the Guardian and the Hero to understand the Romantic attitude toward work, most particularly the 'why bother' aspect. Ideas of how to deal with these attitudes are listed under the section on Mindful Management to follow.

Personal Development for the Romantic

Mind Work: A new idea about power

To move forward, the Romantic needs to progress beyond any vestige of the attitude that 'somebody else should be making life good for me'. It is important that they acknowledge the loss of their birthright to have had all needs met by a caregiver. Once they understand the source of that 'why bother' response in them, the next step is to actively *answer that question*. It is the 'despairing baby' wiring that poses that question. In order to heal this wound, individuals with a Romantic Damsel/Poet thread can remind themselves that – while the wounded baby was helpless – they have an adult and mobile body which can and should move toward making a good life. This conscious dedication can constellate a new wiring that supports agency and success.

'Mobilization of aggression' is the principle for psychotherapeutic work with individuals with Romantic in their personality form. 'Aggression' in this psychological sense can, but does not necessarily, mean anger. The Latin term 'gression' means movement. A particular prefix determines the direction of movement. *Progression* is movement forward. *Digression* is movement to the side. *Regression* is backward movement. The Latin prefix 'ag' means *toward*. Therefore, the literal meaning of 'aggression' refers to our movement *toward* what we want in life. Translated into American, this would be the 'go for it' energy that gets us what we want and need in life.

Romantic Poets and Damsels must mobilize their 'go for it' energy in order to enhance their lives and – if Romantic is a sizeable piece in their personality – strengthen their work ethic.

When the Romantic Damsel/Poet ignites this inner aggressive force they can move into the world to fulfil their own needs. This challenges the assumed reality of helplessness and creates a grounded and genuine independence. Combined with the real sensitivity and openness characteristic of this type, this makes for a kind, accessible personality with a delightfully gentle, relaxed and often playful way of being.

Body Work: Physical fitness is crucial
The Damsel and Poet show the most remarkable response to the right kind of body work. The key issue is low energy due to shallow breathing. When they commit to achieving vigorous fitness, the change can be stunning.

I had a direct experience of the dramatic effect of a committed fitness regime on a person with a very large personality component of Romantic in her personality.

In the late 1990s Ellie came on one of our larger management development programmes at Cranfield University's School of Management. Ellie was a perfect example of the Romantic Damsel type – both for better and for worse. On the positive side she was personally delightful. Her social skills were superb. Wherever she sat at dinner, the conversation was energetic, contactful and amusing. It was probably these lovely social qualities that secured her the rather challenging and high-level job at which she was presently failing. This is the reason she had been put on our programme.

Romantic Poet/Damsel types tend to interview very well. They are typically not nervous, and they thrive on being the centre of attention. Romantics invariably 'talk a good game', and so interviewers are impressed and persuaded. It is when they get into the real work situation that they can fade out and fail to deliver.

This was Ellie's dilemma. She could not do her job well because she ran out of energy. Nevertheless, she was so well liked that her manager invested in sending her on our programme.

Ellie was touched and impressed when she saw the close connection of her developmental story with the Centaur description of what creates a Romantic Poet/Damsel type. Because of this she took to heart the notion that a low energy level can be corrected through physical fitness. She embraced this developmental advice and on returning home after the programme joined a gym and hired a personal trainer.

Seven weeks separated the first and second module of our programme. As I stepped up to the reception desk at the start of module two, I heard a resounding 'Hi Sandy!' behind me. I rightly assumed that this greeting came from a returning delegate. However, when I turned around I was at a loss as to who this strong, high-energy, suntanned young woman was. 'It's me, Ellie!' said the super-charged one. Then I recognized Ellie's face amidst the resilient energy field that surrounded it. 'My personal trainer has declared me fit,' said Ellie, 'and I feel great!'

Ellie's energetic presence was not the only big change. Her issue at work had been literally turned on its head. She had been sent on the programme because she could not meet the remit of her new job. She returned to module two with the *opposite problem*. Now she finished her assigned tasks with time to spare and she regularly complained to her boss that she felt underused and bored.

Ellie is the most dazzling example of how establishing a dedicated fitness regime upgrades the life and work of a Romantic Poet/Damsel, but I have witnessed many more. Physical fitness is good for all of us but for the Romantic it is transformative.

The undermining low-energy issue – whether chronic or in the form of 'energy gaps' – can be dramatically healed through true physical fitness. Get a personal trainer, go to circuit training, take up running or any number of the new offerings to get you moving and breathing.

Because encouragement and support is fundamental to healing this wound, the presence of a personal trainer early on is recommended. In fact, I think it is a good permanent investment. However, invariably once the connection is made between vitality and regular exercise the case will be made. All of us do well with regular physical exercise. For the Romantic Poet/Damsel it is a non-optimal necessity. For them the problem of low energy returns when exercise is forsaken.

The Mindful Management of the Romantic
A simple something that makes them relax: ATTENTION

Finding the balance in what you require of these people is crucial. Too much pressure causes collapse and loss of motivation and not enough encourages laziness.

Romantics will need structured and time-bound objectives. Frequent checking up is very important. Do *not* generalize this management style. Other types would find this attentiveness offensive. Romantic Damsel/Poets often feel supported and motivated by regular supervision. Remember, the original wound was around lack of attention.

There is a genuine lack of energy and stamina. Once this is understood the situation can be handled and the energy level improved by giving Poets and Damsels bite-sized chunks of the task along with concomitant attention when they complete each bit.

This attention should be truthful, direct and respectful. Be tough on laziness, but do it within the (often spoken) context of 'I know you can do better than this', which respects them as a human being even as you give them a hard time as a 'personality'.

When necessary, stronger statements like 'As your boss I *require* you to do your job properly' and even tougher statements like 'If you *want* this job you are going to have to *do* the job' are all helpful. So long as you stay grounded in your respect for them as a person, you can be robust and challenging in the attention you give. After all, we are not respecting human potential by allowing our colleagues to slip out of their responsibilities.

Guardian types should avoid any temptation to rescue these individuals. Support helps but doing the job for them encourages dependency.

Hero types tend to dismiss the Romantic Damsel/Poet as a waste of space. Heroes need to remember that developing their people is as much a part of their job as achieving the task in hand. Their problem with sensitivity can become apparent when they are responsible for more energetically delicate types.

The larger the aspect of Romantic within a personality, the more chronic the energy issues will be. An element of a stronger form (Hero or Guardian) makes a huge difference. Damsel with a stripe of Huntress (Poet/Warrior) is a frequent combination. As mentioned above, it is a pleasant mix often producing a sensitive but energetic individual. When there is a pervasive Damsel or Poet thread there will be a 'why bother?' drop-out point. Then support and challenge will be required.

In conclusion, the Romantic Damsel/Poet type takes time and effort to manage. If done mindfully their development is comparatively simple. Of all of the five types they are the easiest to evolve. What is required is *maturation*.

There is a very young child within that needs to grow up. Handle them well and they will respond and give you the satisfaction of having enhanced your human resource. Knowing when to stop trying is crucial. As a rough guide, Guardian types stay with the effort too long and Hero types give up too soon. Typically, the Magicals do not begin. Of course, as with all the types, if the patterning goes deep, the difficulty will be greater.

Handling the Romantic Client

DO NOT ABANDON, because this type lacks a grounded reality function, adequate, healthy relating will be seen in this light.

They need to hear from you often. Telephone and email and check regularly on how they are. Was the order on time? Is there any feedback on your performance? Are they completely happy? WARNING: If you do this with a Magical Wizard/Sprite, they could think you are a stalker. This approach to a Hero Warrior/Huntress will get you labelled a time waster and a nuisance.

By the way, Romantics are rarely completely happy, so be clear in your own mind what is 'good enough' or they could possibly run you ragged. The Romantic Damsel/Poet carries an unconscious predisposition to be unfulfilled due to babyhood wounds, which they easily and unknowingly transfer into adult life. Be aware of this when you ask the question 'Are we doing enough for you?' But ask the question all the same. They thrive on the reassurance that you care about them personally.

Give your Romantic client a lot of time when you meet personally, and they also really like lunch or dinner – or both!

Approach with social small talk, asking them questions about their lives. These are personable, social individuals who appreciate a good chat and a pleasant time. They are usually rather egocentric so, although they will ask about you, they will quickly want to get back to talking about themselves. This is different from Guardian type who will genuinely want to hear your news and will be offended if you don't give it.

STAGE TWO OF DEVELOPMENT
TODDLERHOOD: The Crucible of Superheroes

As a human baby masters standing and locomotion during the second year of life s/he graduates to the status of toddler. Mothers and fathers will know what a huge difference this change represents in what is required of them to be good parents.

The technological lens of neuroscience reveals that at this time higher centres of the limbic brain light up and new faculties come online that have to do with developing a concept of 'self' and 'other'.

This budding awareness comes straight out of a healthy toddler's mouth. Big new words are 'me', 'mine' and 'no'. Good parenting at this stage both confirms the toddler's growing sense of being 'my own person' while at the same time indicating the effect his or her behaviour has on *other* persons.

We intuitively know that it is futile to appeal to babies to think about the impact of their behaviour on others. I am sure many parents will remember silently pleading with a screaming infant to give them a break and go back to sleep, but – even in the most demented of moments – none would have expected a cooperative response from the baby.

At the toddler stage, evolving capacities for mutuality and interpersonal awareness become the developmental task. Unfolding structures within the brain make this possible. Appropriate growth no longer centres on survival and nourishment but on recognition that there are others in the world and that they need to be taken into account as *subjective individuals* rather than *objective resources or obstacles*. 'Are you for me or against me?' is the stance of the healthy toddler for whom it really is 'all about me'. Good parenting will now be focused on establishing the felt sense of 'other' in the child.

The wholesome worldview good parents seek to establish in the toddler is:

- *I am powerful and deserve to be taken into account.*
- *Others also deserve to be taken into account.*
- *The world is a place of sharing.*

Again, parents will recognize the different skills and attention required in order to install in a baby a sense of safety, security and all that is needed to convince a toddler that a brother or sister has a right to their own toys or play decisions. It is really important to have the 'yes' and 'no', 'good' and 'bad', 'mine' and 'yours' dialogues. They are not easy.

This change of focus is a big shock to the illusion of grandiosity cultivated in the fortunate baby. As a good parent to a toddler, you are required to help your child relinquish the conviction that s/he owns the whole world. As a fortunate baby-turned-robust-toddler, they will fight to retain it.

Failure to achieve the developmental tasks of this phase leads to repercussions later in life and will be found to underpin the unconscious worldview of the Superhero.

THE SUPERHEROES: The Wonder Woman and the Superman

This personality type is formed around the Right to Power which is formative from one to three years of age.

This third formative stage coincides with standing and moving on two feet. There is a big power shift when a little one starts to walk, and neuroscientists confirm that new aspects of the brain come 'online' at this point. Toddlers have far more clout than babies. Supermarkets and department stores abound with frantic young parents rendered impotent by some little person in the midst of the 'terrible twos'.

This phase of development has been brilliantly named 'first adolescence'. Like its pubescent namesake, it is a stormy and harrowing time for parents. Both toddler and teenager are awash in watersheds between life stages. Just as true adolescence marks the juncture between childhood and adulthood, so first adolescence lies in the cross-current between helpless babyhood and childhood.

Somewhere between the ages of three and four, the capacity for cognitive thought is consolidated in the brain. This is when you can make deals with kids that more or less stick. 'If you stop screaming here at the grocery store I will give you a lollipop when we get home' would be such a negotiation and establishing it represents a developmental achievement.

You can *take care* of a baby and truly meet all of its needs. You can *reason* with a child of four or five and make sensible progress toward some common end. The toddler bit in between is difficult. It is here that the battle of wills rightfully belongs and it is truly a battle. Moreover, it is not always certain who will prevail.

The foundation of interpersonal respect needs to be laid down in the psyche during this phase. Now, here is the really unfair bit. If the parenting has been good during babyhood, the job at this stage will be *much harder*. Coming from a generous babyhood, a child enters this phase full to the brim with confidence and energy. A good babyhood is like Paradise. The world meets every need and the baby experiences itself as the omnipotent centre of the universe. Now, as a toddler, s/he can *move around* as well. 'The world is my oyster' is the life stance of the robust one- and two-year-old.

At this stage a good parent instigates the loss of Paradise and a healthy yearling will fight to maintain its power with all the cunning and raw energy of an untamed creature. First adolescence is a period when good parenting approaches an art form.

The kinds of dysfunctions that arise during this phase will be discussed in due course, but if the child does not learn to respect the rights of others, problem behaviours are almost certain later in life. An adult who continues to see the world as his or her oyster is overconfident and too sure of themselves. Their way of being is typically inflated and grandiose. They over-handle the world often to the distress and objection of others.

The image here illustrates the thinking pattern typical of such an adult who has not had their power appropriately limited so as to become sufficiently socialized at the toddler stage of life. It describes a lateral and opportunistic ability to respond quickly and flexibly to whatever occurs with the single focused intent to 'get what I want'. There are benefits to the ability to think in a lateral and flexible mode. However, when paired with a single-minded view of the world as 'my oyster', it can pose a considerable danger to that world and the people in it.

SUPERHERO LATERAL OPPORTUNISTIC THINKING

The Developmental Crucible of the Superheroes

Key perspectives shift as a result of organic changes in the brain when the baby becomes mobile at around eleven months old. New means of self-expression become available during this period – especially important is the ability to walk. There is an exuberant excitement about these new capacities and the increased arena of activity. Psychologists devoted to the study of this period suggest that during this time the child becomes far more attuned to the reactions of others.[5]

A few months after mastering mobility the brain advances its scope and the toddler becomes self-reflective. That is, they can think about themselves and for the first time have an idea of both who they are and how they should be. It is at this point that parents can begin a meaningful dialogue about how to behave. As stated above, this is the field where the battle of wills plays out and, unlike the helpless baby, the toddler is a worthy opponent.

Ideally, having been welcomed and strengthened in babyhood the little human flowers into active expression in the world. Good parenting celebrates the new abilities like walking and talking and at the same time begins to address the omnipotence left over from a generous babyhood, pruning it back in a manner that is kind but also firm.

At this point it is a parent's task to break the news to the powerful toddler that the world must be shared. The Right to Power frames this stage of development and as mentioned elsewhere, the better start you have given your baby the harder job you will have 'taming' your toddler into the accepted social modes necessary for living in the world with others.

As always, additional factors affect this situation. If the genetic temperament of the child is sensitive, shy and introverted s/he will emerge from the most generous of babyhoods with an innate openness to the reactions of others and so present a different challenge than a genetically bold, extrovert child who will be driven by strong impulses fuelled by high energy aimed at impacting on the world outside. This toddler will challenge you more robustly and be quite a draw on your energy and your patience.

The lessons that the now mobile toddler must learn is 'there are limits to my power' and 'for my actions there are repercussions'. At this stage parents must install the social rules of human interaction we all live by in the child's consciousness. For example, 'we do not snatch toys away from other children', and 'we do not bite that other child when s/he will not hand over the desired object'. 'We hold the hand of an adult when we cross the street' and 'we do not take bags of sweets off the shelves of the supermarket to take home with us'.

In the newly emerging, but still primitive, toddler mind the world is split into two camps. I am 'bad' when I scratch my baby brother. I am 'good' when I pick up my toys. Others are also split. 'Good mummy' lets me do what I want. I 'love' her. There is also 'bad mummy' who will not give me what I want. Her, I 'hate'.

There is so much for the toddler to learn and so very much of it is about limitation. The healthy child at this stage is naturally a little hoodlum full of power and not yet limited by socialization. Good parenting is dedicated and consistent in the assertion of boundaries, enabling the growing brain to wire in the basic rules for living together through the emerging aptitude for 'concrete operational thinking'. This is a kind of practically focused 'do this and not that' mode which has none of the rational subtlety of the later developing left brain. Toddlers learn through doing and then experiencing simple concrete and direct responses to their behaviour.

Many readers will know from experience that toddlers do not respond to reason. It is through repeated corrective responses and dedicated consistency on the part of committed (and increasingly exhausted) parents that the toddler comes to learn what is 'good' and 'not good' or 'bad'.

One early June in the south of England I was running a programme in the grounds of a beautiful old country house. We were taking an extended lunch hour because – as often happens in early summer in England – this was the *first* sunny day we had had in months. As I wandered around the property I spotted a small guest house through a hedge that was obviously rented to families on holiday. It had a swimming pool and sitting on the side of the pool was George and his daddy. Both were that bluish-white colour that the English complexion turns through the winter. Both were deeply enjoying those first rays of sunshine on what was clearly the first day of their stay.

As I watched, George picked up a sizeable rock and eyeing the pool lifted his arm ready to throw. 'No, George,' said Daddy. 'We don't throw rocks into the swimming pool.' George paused, but he did not put the rock down. Ten seconds later he proffered a throw once again. Daddy repeated, 'George, do not throw the rock into the pool.' George's arm moved further back, taking on the posture of a javelin athlete ready to launch. 'If you throw the stone into the pool, George, we will go into the house and you will go down for a nap.' I can tell you without any doubt that neither of those blueish bodies wanted to leave the blessed sunlight that early June day. I held my breath and spied on enthralled by the drama. Much was at stake here. The omnipotence of George and the commitment to dutiful parenting of Daddy were facing off. Splash. The rock hit the water. There was a long, long pause. Then, without a word and with admirable dedication to the psychological development of his son, Daddy picked up (the now screaming) George and walked quietly into the dark and chilly cottage.

During the toddler stage, relevant adults need to give the child positive feedback on unfolding achievements, while presenting the bad news about the limitations of reality. Good parenting in this third developmental crucible promotes the continued flowering of self through the wholesome *pruning back* of the now outdated orientation toward omnipotence.

The pruning back of babyhood grandiosity is achieved through a process called 'mirroring'. Adults shape a more social way of being in the world by reflecting back what the child is doing and reacting to it. Good parenting is paying attention to who the child is becoming and facilitating that individuality while at the same time teaching about the rights and needs of others and the social rules of the world. New qualities and competencies are supported and guided but the child is required to express themselves through appropriate interactions and social living. If this pruning and limiting is insufficiently done, the child's sense of her or his right to power will overgrow, like a garden that is not properly weeded. A sense of entitlement will intrude on others and a sense of being 'above the law' will cause difficulty in adult life in both private and work domains.

Things go seriously amiss at this stage if a parent is immature psychologically and in some way uses the child to complete or validate their own identity. A classic scenario is a needy mother who turns to her son for male support and comfort. Often she will indicate or actually say to the boy that he is the 'real' man in the family and that his father is either a 'wimp' or a 'bully' or something equally negative.

The boy gets 'caught up' in a role that is literally and organically beyond him. This is a truly damaging context because – somewhere in his unconscious mind – he registers that in order to be loved, he must *be more than he really is*. Whatever the specific manifestation, the core message that informs the Superhero pattern is 'Be who I need you to be and then I will love you'. The child responds because there is really no other viable choice. In so doing the unfolding ego self lifts off its own unique base and is put at the service of the ego needs of others.

Psychoanalyst Heinz Kohut, who wrote extensively about this crucible, describes this wound as 'tragic'. Deep inside the child concludes, 'If I must be something more than I am in order to be loved, who I really am must not be worthy.' This devastating conclusion is the unconscious core of the superhero pattern, and the central feeling that emanates from it is *humiliation*.

The rivalry engendered within the worst-case scenario pictured above separates son from father by creating distance and disrespect, which is an unspeakable loss. Such a history, along with the resulting Superhero personality form, characterizes a large number of managing directors and CEOs in organizations I have worked with over the years. The unconscious habit of 'rising to the occasion' and 'saving the day' established within this crucible takes the Superhero very far in professional life. It also costs them a great deal in their inner life and in all of their relationships with others. The literal 'hijack' of their growing identity derails an important piece of development that is crucial to grounded and realistic relating to other people.

Theory of Other Minds and the Reality Function

Notice that, as with the baby mind, it is still 'all about me', but, hopefully, *unlike* the baby the toddler has an increasing number of experiences that firmly communicate that others are 'other' and *not under his or her control*. Psychologists refer to this crucial learning as the 'theory of other minds'. This is an important concept in developmental psychology.

This ability to see others as separate and unique with their own rights and needs forms the core of what I am calling a 'reality function'. There is a watershed in psychological development – the 'reality line' – that delineates which of our five types are grounded in conventional, consensual reality. The 'theory of other minds' is such an important developmental achievement that it is worth taking some time and space to really understand it.

Have you ever played a game of hide-and-seek with a two-year-old where, when asked to hide, she puts her hands over her own eyes and cries, 'Ready!'? This is a perfect example of the *absence* of 'theory of other minds'. In the junior toddler's view, because *she* cannot see *you*, *you* cannot see *her*. There is *literally* no mind other than hers. What she knows, sees and thinks is what everyone knows, sees and thinks. Establishing the aptitude to realize that others are separate and know different things, see things differently and think differently is a key learning task for a two-year-old. When this learning is missed out, problems with reality appear in later life.

When raising toddlers, we work at wiring in a 'theory of other minds' by encouraging the growth of 'empathy', that is the capacity to tune into what another person is feeling. Toddler Jack quite naturally 'wants to do what he wants to do' like any two-year-old. Let's imagine that what Jack wants to do is to remove the head from sister Mary's doll. Mary reacts to the beheading with tearful distress. We build empathy in Jack by quietly and steadfastly making him aware of the effect of his actions on Mary. 'Oh, look how sad Mary is to see her dolly hurt. How would you feel if somebody broke your favourite car?' In this way we encourage Jack's now ready and willing brain to 'wire in' a programme geared to imagine – or theorize – what it is like to be that other person. Likewise, when toddler Susie is overzealous in her loving of the family cat, we say, 'How does the kitty feel when you squeeze her so tight? Let's pet her in a nice, quiet way and see if she will purr for us.'

It is good for the helpless baby to believe that the others around him are under his control and have no existence other than to meet his needs. Not feeling the reality of infantile helplessness is a positive illusion we seek to create for a baby. However, it is crucial that this illusion is relinquished during toddlerhood. The big learning task for the two-year-old is to realize that other people are *not* under his or her control and that they have their own wants and needs and rights.

Eighteen months ago my good friend and colleague Nancy asked me to advise her on what to do about the increasing bossiness of her two-year-old daughter, Leah. Leah had taken to shouting instructions at her mother in the manner of a rapid-fire machine gun. 'Mummy come here!', 'Mummy sit down with me!', 'Mummy don't sit there, sit here!', 'Mummy go away!' Nancy's strategy had been to ignore the demands, but that only led to uproar as they were made again at a higher volume. What to do?

Because the toddler thinks of another person as a thing – an object – they will do what many of us do when an object does not comply with our expectations. What is your reaction when a door does not open? Isn't it likely that you will give it another push or two, maybe, if necessary, delivering a brisk kick in order to get the door to meet your expectations and open? Leah's escalation of intensity when ignored was very like this.

Knowing that Leah's developmental task was to begin to see others as separate beings with their own rights, I suggested to Nancy that next time Leah made a demand such as 'Mummy sit down' she look at her firmly and warmly and say, 'Leah, *Mummy does not want* to sit down'. She did exactly this the following day and the impact was striking. When her mother responded to her as a *subject* – with separate feelings and rights – saying, 'Mummy does not want to sit down' Leah stopped short, with a look of utter shock on her little face.

This is how all of us look and feel when the world we know suddenly changes. That moment represented a significant snip in the pruning back of the grandiosity of Leah's generous babyhood when her mother had, indeed, been at her beck and call. This encounter continued with Nancy explaining to Leah that Mummy sometimes needs to do things that mean Leah will have to *wait* because what she wants at the moment is *inconvenient for Mummy*. Through experiences like this Leah will build the capacity to theorize about what might be happening in the mind of another. This is a big and important step in mental and psychological development and not everybody makes it.

When the wiring in of 'theory of other minds' is not achieved, the individual – as a child and later as a grown-up – continues to see others as 'objects'. They are 'resources' or 'obstacles' and respectively 'for me' or 'against me'. They are not separate and complex 'subjects' with their own feelings, thoughts and desires. The 'objectification' of others is a central developmental issue for the Superhero personality, and it is a major complaint regarding their leadership style. Dedicated personal development of the type to be described shortly can address the question of empathy and significantly change the way others are viewed and treated by Superhero Wonder Women and Supermen.

With the development of 'theory of other minds' the evolving child moves past the process of 'splitting' self and others into binary categories of 'good' and 'bad'. The older toddler begins to develop the capacity to tolerate *ambivalence*, realizing that they themselves are both 'good' and 'bad' and that this is also true of others. Mummy does some things I like and some things I do not like but she is always my Mummy. This represents the threshold into the category of 'reason-able child'.

To a greater or lesser extent, the Superhero personality does not make this transition to the tolerance of ambiguity. Wonder Woman and Superman are typically not very reasonable with others or themselves. As a result, they tend to have harsh and unrealistic expectations of what they can and ought to do. In their inner life Superheroes remain relentlessly either 'good' or 'bad'. As a result, they can be ruthlessly hard on themselves if they do not achieve what they conceive of as 'good', which invariably has a perfectionistic and superhuman flavour to it. Any achievement other than 'the top' is devastating. Typically, they will call on their lateral and wide-ranging thinking in order to *reposition* things in their favour. Most times they succeed, frequently sacrificing others to save themselves. If unsuccessful at this 'rewriting of history' they may suffer an awful fall into a feeling of worthlessness.

I remember a delegate from some years ago confiding to me and to the members of his small development group that his father always said to him, 'Mark, there is no such thing as second place.' We knew from an earlier recounting of his childhood that as a toddler Mark's feisty, macho attitude had been fanned and inflated by both of his parents rather than being contained and grounded. The harsh and competitive 'chip' on his father's shoulder was firmly installed in toddler Mark, taking hold of his growing identity.

The imprinting of this superhuman remit on his boyhood drove this hard-working man into terrible inner pain in adult life. He recounted a story of a project to which he had given all his considerable flair and daring but which had not proved successful. We were all touched and impressed with his efforts. Fellow group members proposed the healthy attitude that as he had given it 'his best shot' he had been – despite the outcome – a *success as a person*.

This higher and more rational level of discrimination was not possible for our Superman. He got up from his chair and walked to the side of the room and with his back to us silently rested his head on the wall in the terrible grip of that most awful feeling of humiliation. 'Superhero or Zero' is a way to capture what happens in the inner life of this personality type when they cannot be 'on top'. The only other place is the 'nowhere' of shame and humiliation.

In the classic distortion of this third crucible, a parent takes possession of the child's future. In the service of this, the wholesome pruning of the natural grandiosity of babyhood is ignored and the tendency toward omnipotence is encouraged. In the image shown here this process is pictured in the huge size of the ego circle when compared with the ideal. The Superhero personality over-blooms into an inflated, self-entitled way of being because of these two factors.

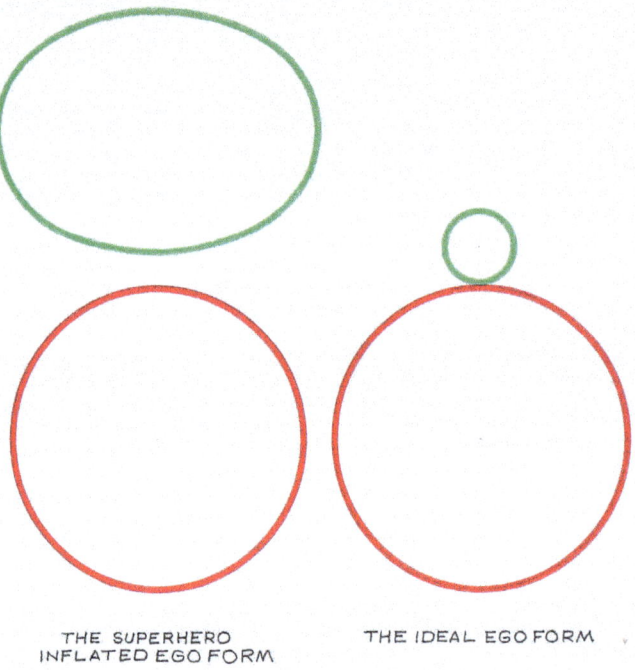

THE SUPERHERO INFLATED EGO FORM

THE IDEAL EGO FORM

A false and inflated self – created to meet the needs of a parent – is *disconnected* from the natural potential SELF. This inflated self must then be maintained at all costs because self-worth is now based on achieving this unreal and superhuman remit. The Superhero maintains an over-expanded self through an awesome will and highly developed intuition, both of which are forged within this crucible.

Because the emergent ego of the Superhero has been hijacked by the needs of parents there is no access to deeper inner resources for support when things do not work out in the outside world. Looking at the ego pattern of the Superhero – disconnected from access to the deeper resources of the inner SELF – we can imagine how dependent they are on the applause of the world. In that gap between the inflated ego circle and the circle containing the deeper inner life lies despair. This image gives us insight as to why Superheroes are so driven to be on top and can be so ruthless and even dangerous when they feel threatened with a fall.

In the introductory case study, Hero manager Peter is unaware of Superhero Patrick's characteristic hunger for approbation. Had he been able to give Patrick's ego a craved-for boost of applause, he (Patrick) may well have relaxed and performed rather than becoming disengaged and unpredictable. But such ego boosts must not be inflationary or mere flattery. That repeats the original wound. Finding something realistic and truthful to say that provides a lift to self-esteem and self-importance is what will be genuinely helpful.

That is not too much to ask. Each personality has a simple 'need' arising from a central wound that is the core of the type. For the Magical Wizard/Sprite this need is for 'acceptance', a sense of safety. For the Romantic Damsel/Poet it is 'attention', a sense that I am not alone. For the Superhero Wonder Woman/Superman it is a moment of 'applause' that boosts an inwardly tenuous self-esteem. Providing a context where others can deliver their best is part of good leadership. More about how to do this with a Superhero type is outlined in detail under the heading of Mindful Management.

Although they typically lack empathy, Superheroes have an uncanny intuition regarding the thoughts and needs of others, which is key to their remarkable political acuity. It seems like they can 'read your mind'. Reviewing the situation that forms them, we can understand why their political reading of situations is so adept. The very nature of this crucible is political. The parental environment signals 'Be who I need you to be and then I will love you.' In order to get the love and attention needed to grow and develop, a child in this context must 'read the minds' of important others around them so s/he can 'be what is wanted' and so be loved. It can be no surprise that their political skills are well honed. They started practising them at the age of two.

We can understand the body pattern of the Superhero Wonder Woman/Superman in the context of that formative message, 'Be who I need you to be and then I will love you'. The child rises to the occasion emotionally and also physically. They literally pull and *hold* themselves *up* above their simple humanness to meet the needs of the loved one. The Superhero body is characterized by an inflated chest and massive shoulders.

The shoulders and chest operate like a fused unit, producing an overbearing presence even if the individual is not particularly tall. Often the lower body is notably less developed than the upper torso and seems not to match it. This is especially true of the legs. The seaside postcard character of the macho beach-bully with a huge chest and skinny legs is a cruel and extreme reference to this form.

The second key physical feature is a forceful piercing quality to the eyes. This may be standard or flash out when the Superhero takes a stand about whose will shall prevail. This 'power gaze' is the hallmark of the *hold up* energetic pattern. Tension in the eye area is a definitive characteristic of only two of the five types: The Magical (Wizard/Sprite) and Superhero (Superman/Wonder Woman). However, the quality and meaning of these gazes are very different. In Magicals, the look is like that of a rabbit frozen in the headlights.

"HOLDING UP" AGAINST THE FEELING OF HUMILIATION

Their energetic charge recoils from contact (frozen stare) and flees away from the world (dissociated spaced-out gaze.) Remember, Magical individuals hold themselves together against the shattering force of fear. The Superhero *hold up* gaze *looks down on* and *deeply into* the world so as to master it and bend it through a force of will into the desired shape. Emerging from a formative environment where s/he had to intuit what was needed, the Superhero habitually and unconsciously reads what is wanted and then uses that information to achieve their personal agenda.

In a pure *hold up* Superhero form, the jaw is massive and square. Energetically, there is an overly free aggressive flow due to lack of realistic parameters at that crucial point in their formative development. Classically, this forms a jutting over-square and bold, even coarsened, jaw and face.

These physical characteristics of inflated chest, piercing gaze, and powerful jaw produce the compelling and powerful physical presence of the Superhero Wonder Woman and Superman.

The Superhero Worldview

On the basis of perceived reality, the Superhero Wonder Woman/Superman mind concludes:

- *I am (or must be) the biggest and the best.*

- *Others are (I need them to be) less than me.*

- *The world is my oyster.*

The Superhero at Work

Both Magical and Romantic personality types stem from scars in babyhood. This early damage leads to a weakening of psychological robustness. Both have a delicacy, even fragility, about them. Neither is particularly realistic, although it should be said here that the spiritualizing of the former and the romanticizing of the latter can be quite attractive characteristics in the right context.

By comparison, the Superhero colleague is typically larger than life, with a huge, even overwhelming, psychological presence. They tend away from the intellectual and the rational, although they can be very bright. They are highly intuitive, and they work from a gut feeling about what is going on. They can make big shifts and changes in direction that unnerve and exasperate other types, which is not infrequently their intent. They often possess a remarkable gift for strategic thinking and an uncanny ability to read political situations. They sense immediately who is in power and what others want and they know how to use this awareness to their own advantage. They typically manoeuvre themselves into the right place at the right time and know precisely what to say to move events their way. They frequently have great charisma and this overstated way of being brings them considerable success in organizational life. Superheroes frequently hold positions of high leadership.

Nevertheless, this adept tuning into others comes at the expense of losing track of their own deeper nature. The growing ego here forsakes the deeper SELF within and makes itself according to the inflated remit of others. In doing this they can lose touch with their own depth, becoming dependent on the applause and approbation of others as a validation of their worth. In the midst of takeovers and down-sizing, it is often those at the top who lose their positions. When this happens to a Superhero Wonder Woman or a Superman they are in psychological danger because so much of their identity depends on the approbation and accoutrements of their position in the world.

As the name suggests, Superheroes are driven to be superhuman. They always seek the top position. This may be done in a gentle or a coercive manner but their control is always definite and complete. In a softer mode the Superhero is often seen as a 'saviour' who controls through protection, sheltering the team from the world at large like a medieval baron would protect the serfs in his fiefdom. The Magical and the Romantic, who are motivated by protection and attention respectively, can do well with this type of leadership. However, stronger ego types, like the Guardian and the Hero, feel insulted and offended if a leader takes a protective position, which seems to them both disrespectful of their strength and patronizing.

I met a fabulous saviour Wonder Woman on one of my programmes at Cranfield University some decades ago. On completion of the day of teaching on the Centaur model, Daisy approached me with tears in her eyes. 'At last I understand myself', she confided. And then she told me her story. She was the first child born to profoundly deaf parents who valiantly wished to have a normal family life together. From the time she was two, Daisy was allocated the task of 'being the ears' of her parents by signalling to them when the telephone or doorbell rang. Far too young she was asked to undertake responsibilities that were beyond the natural unfolding of a toddler.

We can imagine how the Superhero form would arise within this crucible. Out of love, little Daisy would have shifted her focus from her own unique developmental task and instead tuned into what was needed by the beloved others. This fundamental shift of agenda to the outside world is at the core of the developmental history of the Superhero form. What was needed from Daisy was more than a toddler can easily and naturally deliver. In this way, her toddler grandiosity was exploited – albeit not on purpose – and her growing ego went into inflation.

Once wired up to do the 'impossible', Daisy continued under that remit for the rest of her life. Early on she entered a career in public service where she committed her unstoppable energy to the protection and care of others. When I met her Daisy was a well-known and beloved public servant respected for her tireless campaigning for the rights of the needy. To that cause, she sacrificed a private life and was frequently on the edge of exhaustion. It was insight into the source of that relentless drive within her that brought tears of relief to her eyes on my programme at Cranfield.

I have always hoped that, with the insight she gained through Centaur with us, Daisy allowed herself to be more relaxed with her calling – less superhuman – and to give herself some ordinary human self-care while following what was clearly her professional destiny to help others.

Many of her colleagues loved working for and with Daisy. The softer 'saviour' style can produce an inspiring – albeit not particularly planned and rational – context in which others thrive. Nobody thrives and everybody suffers under the leadership of the hard or coercive Superhero Wonder Woman/Superman who operates in 'tyrant' mode. They are often seen as effective by those above them because they 'get the job done'. Moreover, they are adept at positioning things so they look good, while those who work for them are frequently in distress. At their worst, this harsh tyrant type dominates and even humiliates peers and staff.

Personal value for the Superhero is rooted in being on top. That is why traditionally – as seen in comic books and movies – neither Superman nor Wonder Woman *ever have an equal*. If the Superhero is to remain on top, able colleagues or up-and-coming talent must be cut down to a lesser size. In the case of the hard or coercive Superhero, this process can be both ruthless and unethical. Tips for Guardians and Heroes on how to avoid this are listed under the Mindful Management heading at the end of this section.

For the Superhero – whether the soft 'saviour' or the hard 'tyrant' – 'the end always justifies the means' and the end is to always be on top. With such a remit, this form of personality is fundamentally unrealistic. It is a different kind of unreality than that of Magical Wizard/Sprite or the Romantic Damsel/Poet. It is tougher and more convincing. However, despite their deeply ingrained political dexterity, the Superhero can make disastrous mistakes when they focus so much on power and position and lose sight of practical circumstances.

Gifts of the Superhero
Charisma – They are often truly exciting and inspiring leaders. In the softer 'saviour' form they are frequently committed to a positive cause and give a great deal to others in their drive to be superhuman.

Strategy – They are politically adroit and when this is used positively, it can be a great advantage to their team and organization as well as to themselves.

Success – This type is the one most frequently found at the top of organizations and they are also frequently found at the head of autocratic nations.

The Superhero Shadow

Domineering – They control and undermine others who could be equals.

Scheming – They manoeuvre for personal power. This is not infrequently at a cost to others or the task at hand or the overall good of the organization.

Ruthless – The end justifies the means. In extreme cases this can go beyond what is actually legal and/or fundamentally moral.

What the Superhero Brings

As energy level is built in a child through interaction and stimulation, it is easy to understand how the Superhero history would promote and maintain a high energetic charge. However, their most remarkable gift is their reflexive strategic skill. They read the political situation with incredible ease and this enables them to move quickly up the organizational ladder driven by their need to be on top and in control. We have discussed the source of this gift within the formative crucible. Because love is dependent upon meeting the needs of others, intuition becomes highly attuned. 'Be who I need you to be and then I will love you' is actually a political contract. The Superhero personality has been operating strategically since the second year of life. No wonder they are so good at it.

Both the gift of charisma and that of strategy may be used to positive or negative ends. Both need to be grounded in reality and goodness or we get dreadful happenings where innocent people lose their money or even their lives having trusted a charismatic but unrealistic leader. This grounding can take place through relationships with realistic colleagues but ideally the Superhero will seek to reconnect with the deeper aspects of their own nature through the 'examined life' proposed by Socrates and engaged in by many on a personal-development path.

Because this is such a powerful type, the difference between character style (healthy) versions and more distorted forms is great. The best of the Superheroes provide some of the positive inspirational leaders of our day.

They are exciting and frequently take us beyond where we believe we can go. We need their flair and daring. However, organizational life and the world generally suffer from an overabundance of narcissism and entitlement, which are key features of this type.

Limiting Attitudes of the Superhero

The Superhero literally loses track of their true SELF. The false grandiose self created to rise to the occasion of parental need is all they have. It must, therefore, be protected at all costs. 'The end justifies the means' is a fundamental Superhero attitude. When this attitude is activated it can lead to harsh and ruthless behaviour. It is habitual for Superheroes to ask more than is possible of themselves and in this way, they project the dynamics of their formative scenario into their current life. *I must be on top! I must be in control! I must win! I should always know what to do!*

They rely primarily on intuition which fuels abilities to duck and dive and wheel and deal. Superheroes infuriate more logical, rational types with statements like 'Don't distract me with the facts!'

The remit to be superhuman can take many forms, but it always requires that 'others are inferior to me'. In this regard, the softer Superhero type often operate as a benign dictator controlling through protection. Harsher forms are coercive and tyrannical, exercising control through domination and humiliation.

Your loyalty is vital to the Superhero personality and their definition of loyalty is characteristically unrealistic and egocentric. You are expected to do their bidding and think their thoughts without question. Their attitude is 'You are either with me or against me.' In this way other people are objectified. The Superhero personality sees those they work with as either resources or extensions of themselves rather than separate complex beings. When a personality contains more realistic threads like Guardian or Hero this tendency will be less. Therefore, a dash of the Superhero thread in these more grounded and moral types can produce a fabulous leadership profile.

Their own self requirement puts a great deal of pressure on these individuals and thence on all those who work with them. At their best Superheroes challenge convention and limitation and their drive can produce remarkable results. We cannot do without them. Looking at the famous leaders from World War Two we get a spread of Superhero expression. Winston Churchill and Franklin D.

Roosevelt were 'character style' superheroes. Hitler, Mussolini and Stalin were 'neurotics' (perhaps even 'character disorders') of the same type.

Personal Development for the Superhero

Mind Work: A new idea about others

Above all, the Superhero needs to consider the possibility that there is more to life than power. Only when they acknowledge that they are missing something of value will they consider changing their 'winning formula'. When they let themselves realize that other people see, hear and feel one another in ways that produce real joy and love of life, then their yearning for genuine human relating may take them in search of their deeper potentials. The journey is a hard one. When they relinquish their ego inflation, they meet an awkward child-self who had to be some kind of 'big deal' too early in order to be acceptable.

In the commitment to take up this inner task, the Superhero challenges the assumed reality that who they really are – without the performance – lacks value. The Superhero engaged in the search for their deeper SELF needs every bit of their awesome will and determination to retrieve their true identity. The encouraging news is that in discovering their real self they will not lose their power or archetypal gifts of charisma and daring and lateral thinking. These will be given added dimension as they embrace their natural human vulnerability and become better grounded in authentic human relating.

On their journey, Superheroes will need others who will support and respect the emergent, and at first delicate, self-expression rather than the grandiose inflated self. This trust of others is healing because it challenges their assumed reality that people relate to one another only on the basis of mutual use.

Body Work: finding the 'ground'

Good body work for those who energetically *hold up* is anything that helps them *let down* out of the inflated chest into lower body and legs. These are metaphors for the deeper SELF and grounded reality respectively. The gentle martial art of t'ai chi or vigorous walks and non-competitive environments are helpful, as is any sport played purely for pleasure.

Meditation is not an easy option for the overactive Superhero Wonder Woman/Superman but it does make sense within their growth needs. Competitive sports may be good for them in some ways, but they tend to hype a Superhero back into the 'I'm on top' mode and so – while always good for physical fitness – they are less helpful in a self-development regime.

The Mindful Management of the Superhero
A simple something that makes them relax: APPLAUSE

Boundaries are crucial. Clearly demonstrate your space and theirs. This is easier managing downward than managing upward or managing colleagues but it must be done in all cases.

When setting boundaries or limits, begin with a positive statement acknowledging their power. 'You are in charge; I understand that…', 'You are the boss…' or for staff 'I value your energy and determination or skill…'. Remember that position and power are the prime motivators of this personality type. They need to feel their power base acknowledged before they let their guard down. Find a way to give them what they need to relax but *do not flatter*. Untruth cheapens everyone.

These individuals are wily and consciously or unconsciously they register manipulation. Being used was the key wound so it is both bad management and wrong action to repeat it. Find a truth with which you can honestly approach them. Whatever you may think of somebody's leadership style, if they are your boss that is a fact you can truthfully acknowledge. Give them their rightful position and they may well give you yours.

The Hero Warrior/Huntress personality can have great difficulty with this. Often they insist they will not be managed by anyone they do not respect and they rarely relate positively to a Superhero's irrational and lateral thinking. The Hero values logic and fairness and the Superhero is based on intuition, cultivated emotionality and opportunism. Nevertheless, the *truth is always dignified* and it is often necessary to acknowledge and register respect for the *position* despite who is in it. Guardians may also disapprove of a Superhero leadership style but they are by second nature less confrontational as are Magicals and Romantics. Please note: real infringements of morality or the law are, of course, another matter.

Avoid head-on collisions. Heroes beware – the Superhero thinks constantly about position and winning. If you worry them they move into attack and can become dangerous.

They are natural politicians – stay aware. Help them access their strategic capacity for the good of the team or the company. Remember, the character style or softer version often sacrifices much personal pleasure and satisfaction to meet their superhuman remit. Frequently, organizations and teams gain from their inner drive to be more than an ordinary human being. But be aware: if you get in the way or become a liability, you will be sacrificed.

You need to know that winning and position is often more important to them than the task. Often, the more neurotic Superman or Wonder Woman will sacrifice the success of the team to consolidate personal position.

Along with Magicals, the Superhero is the hardest personality type to manage but it is necessary to do so. This includes managing upward. If you do not draw boundaries you encourage bad behaviour. Both consciously and unconsciously Superheroes seek colleagues they can trust and when well-managed, they provide a valuable resource that can border on brilliance. Unmanaged, they can be loose cannons.

Handling the Superhero Client

Treat them royally. Because this type lacks a firm reality function, adequate, healthy relating will be seen as inadequate and disrespectful.

Let them know how important their business is to you or your company.

Do not lie or flatter as that disrespects both you and them. Rather focus on the simple truth that you value their patronage and mean to give them the best service possible anywhere. May I stress again the notion of *patronage*.

Make yourself aware of the successes they have achieved and mention these on a regular basis. This need not be creepy. Your Superhero Wonder Woman/ Superman client must know you are aware of her or his position. You can repeat stories of past glories because this type operates via personal myth. The fact that you add to it will stand you in good stead.

Be aware that this behaviour would get you disliked by Guardians and Heroes and despised by Magicals.

Approach bearing gifts – take them out, demonstrate their value by honouring them. A Hero client will be fine with a sandwich in your office over lunch. In most cases you are ill-advised to do that with a Superhero. The Ritz for lunch is a better idea. Superheroes need to know and feel their position of power with you and when they do they are more likely to feel comfortable and well-disposed to what you have to offer.

STAGE THREE OF DEVELOPMENT
THE 'REASON-ABLE' CHILD: The Crucible of Guardians and Heroes

Up until the age of three the right brain, which totally defines babyhood, remains dominant. As a child advances through the third year of life, another area of the brain comes to the fore called the 'new brain' or the neocortex. The neocortex houses the singular human capacity for reflective thinking.

Between three and six years of age the capacity to think rationally establishes within the left brain and by the end of this stage the logical, linear and language aspects of the left hemisphere come into their own and the left brain dominates functioning. The Guardian Earth Mother/Good Father and the Hero Warrior/Huntress personality types develop during this phase of the formative years when a cogent grasp of the social rules of living with others along with a capacity to reason become possible.

THE GUARDIANS: The Good Father and the Earth Mother

This personality type is created around the Right to Freedom which is formative between two and a half and four years of age.

The Developmental Crucible of the Guardian
Healthy children are like young animals. They need to move and shout and play hard.

Freedom in this context is the right:

- *to explore the world as a non-expert*
- *to adventure to the very edge of the realistic limits established in toddlerhood*
- *to fall down, dust off and begin again*
- *to interact passionately (but not violently) with peers*
- *to straightforwardly (but respectfully) respond to grown-ups.*

Loving but over-cautious or strict and over-controlling parents can impinge upon this natural freedom. Bringing a little human into awareness of society and the rights of others is crucial, however, social consideration and 'what the neighbours think' or what is conventionally acceptable can become too important an issue. What is 'nice', 'polite' and 'proper' may be too much in the minds of parents and so take prominence over affirming the child's right to be passionately alive.

The Guardian crucible both follows on from and reflects back upon that of the Superhero. In a typical scenario, the babyhood has been good and therefore the basic energy level is high and the physical form is robust. During the toddler stage, boundaries have been established and the rights of others have been impressed upon the child. The omnipotence, which was the gift of a generous babyhood, has been trimmed back so as to fit in with social living with other people.

The thinking pattern of the Guardian Good Father/Earth Mother reflects the maturity and mutuality of this personality type. The image here shows how various 'actions' – represented by the circles that expand into the world – originate in the feeling function of the heart. Guardians take others into account and their initiations into the world are evaluated against a code of propriety and courtesy that is at the very least realistic and at best kind. 'Why don't we do X,' a Guardian might say, and then 'But let's check whether everybody is on board before we go ahead.' Or 'How about trying Y with that client, but first let's find out if that fits with their culture.' And so it goes on.

GUARDIAN RELATIONAL THINKING

The Guardian Good Father/Earth Mother thinking pattern, along with that of the Hero (to be explored next) are organized and consistent, reflecting a psychological robustness and maturity based on the firm integration of 'theory of other minds' within their psychological wiring.

Emotional care and respect for others laid down at this stage of development in the personality of the Guardian Good Father/Earth Mothers make them a crucially valuable asset in management and leadership. Others feel emotionally safe with these strong and grounded individuals who often run their teams like a family.

However, within the crucible of the Guardian child the concern for the rights of others can be overdone or sometimes become oppressive. This is what causes the Guardian wound and it is the source of their developmental issue, which is lack of self-assertion. In these typically loving families a barrage of social instructions can dam up the flow of the child's passionate life. The necessary 'socialization' process that is the parental task with the toddler hardens here into a wounding context of 'over-civilization' where all too often passion and independence are sacrificed on an altar of propriety and public opinion. Statements like 'be good, behave, be nice,' 'don't show off' and 'don't be rude', capture the flavour of the family atmosphere from which the Guardian personality emerges.

A developmental problem within the Superhero crucible is the *failure to prune back* natural exuberance, which leads to an over blooming of form that is narcissistic and lacking in awareness of others. The *opposite* is the case for the Guardian Good Father/Earth Mother personality. Here the emergent passion of the little creature is, to some extent, squelched, inhibited and pushed down in order to ensure that the child matches with the expectations of others.

At this stage, the ego/agency aspect of the personality crests into a cutting edge that seeks to hone itself in rational interaction with other egos.

Children want to argue, question and debate, making use of the capacity of their wonderful left brain, which is coming into ascendance.

Having experienced and internalized the social boundaries regarding living with others, the child becomes ready to express a unique and independent self into the world. However, in the crucible of the Guardian, this cutting edge is – in some way and to some extent – denied and a squelching or flattening of agency occurs that wounds the natural, forthright expression of assertion. This squelching of natural assertion is pictured below.

The Guardian ego is the closest of any so far to the ideal form. The image here shows the ego of the Earth Mother/Good Father as consolidated and strong (compared respectively to the Magical and Romantic ego forms) reflecting a 'good enough' babyhood. It is both connected to the deeper SELF and appropriate in size (thanks to proper limiting of toddler grandiosity).

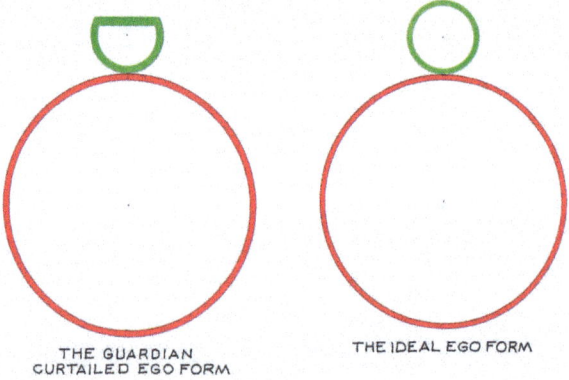

THE GUARDIAN CURTAILED EGO FORM

THE IDEAL EGO FORM

There is always a battle of wills during the toddler stage as the child and parents wrestle with the issue of how life will be lived in the family home. As discussed previously, it is important that the toddler loses some of these battles and so relinquishes the grandiosity of babyhood. However, it is also important that the child does not lose *too many* battles and thence feel defeated in his or her pursuit of psychological independence. In the Guardian crucible, the fight for freedom of expression and psychological independence is – to a greater or lesser extent – compromised. The care of and/or obedience to others is prioritized.

At this point there is more ego strength and agency than ever before and the child resists the denial of this right for a time. But the parents inevitably win.

Frequently there is a history of tantrums. In the end capitulation is inevitable. The adults are twice his or her size and have ultimate power.

However, just below the surface of the well-behaved, nice Guardian lies a reserve of passionate anger at having to give up their unique sense of independence. This may be why Guardians are often drawn to fight for the rights of those who are at an unfair advantage against more powerful forces. The Good Father and Earth Mother often take up the cause of those who are in need of protection, are trodden upon or seen as underdogs.

Taking care of less powerful others by fighting for their rights is a way the Guardian Good Father/Earth Mother live out their unconscious suppressed anger within the rule of 'put others first'. As managers they are steadfast protectors of their teams.

As outlined above, the Guardian personality 'holds in' archaic anger stemming from this denial of the right to freedom and a crushing pressure to please others rather than express themselves. Energetically, anger surges from the pelvis up the back and out the arms and legs and throat in punches, kicks and strong sounds respectively. The block to anger is comprised of networks of powerful muscular tension in the shoulders and the pelvis that stops this flow.

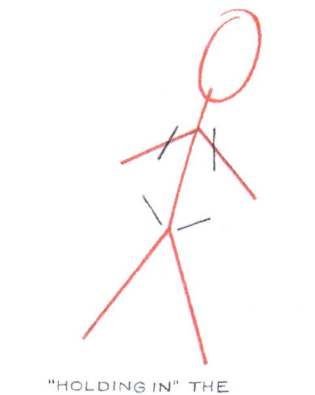

"HOLDING IN" THE EXPRESSION OF FORBIDDEN ANGER

As a result, the shoulders of the Guardian are powerfully curved downward in the interest of 'putting a lid' on all this upward surging passion. Romantic shoulders are also rounded *but they are not strong*. The shoulders of the Guardian grow muscular and strong with the unconscious effort of blocking their forbidden passion and aliveness.

Mirroring the shoulder tension, the pelvis is squeezed forward in order to block the same outward aggressive flow of energy, creating a flatness in the area of the buttocks. This shape notoriously does not 'anchor' work jeans successfully in place and the result is picturesquely referred to as 'builder's bottom'.

So, at both ends of the torso there is a squeezing tension that limits free energetic expression. This is shown in the diagram above. The neck of the Good Father/Earth Mother is typically short and wide in a physical expression of the injunction 'don't stick your neck out'.

On the other hand, the chest area is free of any blocking – in stark contrast to the Hero Warrior/Huntress type to be seen next. A relaxed openness and warmth of a free and available heart is typical of the healthy character-style of the Guardian Good Father/Earth Mother personalities. This heartfelt warmth is reflected in the eyes, which are warm and kind with more liveliness and outgoing energy than the beautiful, dreamy and appealing eyes of the Romantic Damsel/Poet.

Overall, the Guardian body is full of energetic charge, sensuous with vitality and generous in proportion. 'Energy' in this sense is *not* a metaphor. It is substantial. When it is blocked it literally becomes 'substance'. The Guardian torso may be shaped like a circle or a soft-cornered rectangle. Even when this body is perfectly fit there will typically be broadness in the waist.

Like the Superhero, the Guardian Good Father/Earth Mother often has a battle with excess weight but from a very different basis. In the Superhero form it is as if the body physically responds to the mental introjections to 'be a big deal'. In the Guardian form the extra weight is literally the physical manifestation of unlived power and life.

When the Guardian Good Father and Earth Mother successfully address their block to assertion and begin 'speaking out' they frequently lose weight. This is firstly due to being in 'flow' rather than blocked as they *move out* what is on their mind rather than holding it in. Moreover, a changed attitude regarding the expression of anger, to be discussed below, makes 'comfort eating' less necessary. Eating heavy carbohydrates can smother the feeling of anger which is so unacceptable to the Guardian ego.

Finally, the jaw of the Guardian Good Father/Earth Mother does not thrust forward as is the case with more aggressively free patterns of the Superhero and the Hero. It is rounded in shape, broad and soft and held tight as if biting back any anger that would like to be expressed.

Because of the block to assertion and independence, the Guardian Good Father/Earth Mother unconsciously seeks the approval of others, particularly authority figures. They typically comply with the rules. Because of the derailing of the right to independent thinking, they can become anxious when in disagreement with the powers that be. Yet, as explored above, under the surface there is an unconscious objection to any perceived lack of personal respect and in certain circumstances the flip side of the compliant 'nice guy' steps out and you are facing the 'rebel' who can be explosive, disruptive and very, very stubborn.

George in our introductory case study was on the edge of this rebellion when he reacted to the perceived 'pushy' and, for him, 'disrespectful' approach of manager, Peter. He became silently angry and moody instead. Psychologists call this 'passive aggression'. These moods based on perceived impingements can build into a bomb inside a Guardian and then suddenly and unexpectedly explode, causing upset all round. Often most distressed is the Guardian, who will be shocked when s/he can no longer 'hold in' this mounting resource of unexpressed protest.

The Guardian pattern develops during a stage of brain development when the capacity for learning the rules and adapting to the ways of the social world is completely online. So, also, is the newer capacity for rational thinking that checks in with the increased dominance of the left brain. Between three and four years of age a child will naturally want to question the rules and, in so doing, clarify and own the new left brain capacity to reason and argue. This requires very different responses from parents than those needed in the making of limits and boundaries during the toddler stage.

Consider this example: It is eight o'clock on a Monday evening and bedtime for your four-year-old. You say, 'Jimmy, it is time for you to go to bed.' You are tired and on edge after a long day and want to settle down with a glass of wine and watch some relaxing TV. 'Why do I have to go to bed?' asks Jimmy with a mixture of rebellion and complaint in his voice. Can you feel the impulse in you to rejoin, 'Because I said so'? I am sure you can sense that this is not the optimal response even as I hope you can admit that it is a real temptation.

Jimmy is four and he has already learned the hard and fast rules so crucial to the previous stage of development. He knows 'I never go into the road', 'I do not bite my sister' and 'I do not slap Mummy when she says I have to pick up my toys'. These black-and-white, non-negotiable rules pre-date the move over to the left brain where the capacity to reason and think logically reside. At four Jimmy is beginning to exercise agency and articulate an argument.

As a parent your job now is to engage and help him develop this capacity. Swallowing down the 'Because I said so' response you say, 'You have nursery school tomorrow. You don't want to be tired for nursery school.'

'I won't be tired,' Jimmy reassures you. (A frayed parent at this point may well wish she had gone the 'Because I said so' route.)

'Now, Jimmy,' you persevere, 'remember last Friday how sleepy you were in the morning after you stayed up late on Thursday? We don't want that again, do we?'

'I wasn't tired that day at all,' Jimmy maintains.

'Jimmy,' you say, bringing in his favourite teacher, 'remember how Mrs Harris said that you had an upset with Julie over who would help clean the hamster cage? She said you were not your usual helpful self that day and I think that was because you went to bed late on Thursday.'

And so it goes on. In the end you can always pull a 'Mummy card'. Within the framework of logic it is perfectly valid for you to stipulate, 'Jimmy, this is my house and in my house bedtime is eight o'clock for people of four. *When you grow up and you have your own house you can stay up as late as you want.*' The 'my house, my rules' argument definitely has a rationale to it and it is good to have it in reserve when you really need your glass of wine and a little TV.

Can you see how the exchange recounted above encourages rational argument and logical thinking? At four years old the left brain is ready for it, craves it. Imposing the rule *without explanation* does not stimulate the growth of this kind of independent and interactive thought. This cutting edge of interactive dialogue and the brain development it stimulates can get closed down in loving but over-controlled households. Children grow strong through the earlier formative years only to have the cutting edge of ego agency pushed down or even squashed.

In the previous toddler phase the crucial wiring in of 'for your actions there are repercussions' lays down the basic rules of mutual respect for others so essential to social living together. Parenting can remain too long on this track.

Instead of responding to the budding left brain hunger for rational interaction, independent thinking and natural assertion can be foreclosed. This happening is pictured in the previously shown ego image of the Guardian personality with its flattened upper edge where independent and assertive dialogue emerges.

The Guardian Worldview

On the basis of perceived reality, the Guardian Good Father/Earth Mother mind concludes:

- *I will be a good and loving person.*
- *Others have a right to my help.*
- *The world ought to be a good place for people to live in.*

The Guardian at Work

This personality is the most practical and down to earth of all. They are responsible and reliable in completing tasks. They have an enormous energetic resource and are able to work day and night throughout a crisis with effectiveness. They are reliable under pressure; in fact they often require pressure to get themselves going. If there is not enough to do, they may create pressure by consciously or unconsciously leaving things until the last minute. Then, when the heat is on, they hit their stride. Guardians thrive on lots to do and loads going on.

Guardians genuinely care about others. Human warmth and kindness frequently inform their relationships. They are relaxed with people and they find it easy to see the other side in discussions and arguments. This capacity to be understanding and generous with others is a key asset in their managerial style.

Typically, they are responsive to family needs, love their children and strive for a balance between home and work. Because of their interpersonal ease, when they make the shift into management they have a much smoother time than the Magical Wizard/Sprite, who is afraid of people, or the Romantic Damsel/Poet, who tends to avoid responsibility.

The biggest problem the Guardian manager faces is a block to assertion at some level. They typically do not want to upset anybody so being straightforward with corrective criticism or disagreement can be difficult. In such cases they may use their capacity for understanding to *avoid* taking a necessary and fair stand with team members who, for example, do not pull their weight. This can create a sense of injustice which undermines team morale.

Saying 'no' is particularly hard for Guardians and their natural generosity can be exploited – consciously or unconsciously – by less energetic types. Romantic Damsel/Poets are typical culprits here. Their unconscious attitude that 'the big strong people should take care of me' can on occasion team up with the Guardian Good Father/Earth Mother programming to care for others in a 'symbiosis' that is not good for either person. The Guardians get exhausted and the Romantics remain fixed in an immature understanding of the 'give and take' of relationship, which is 'you give – I take'.

At work the Guardian may take on too much and get overloaded with work that isn't actually their responsibility. When they become overburdened in this way they may begin to feel negative about the situation and go into a 'victim' or 'martyr' mode. Their wiring to be a 'nice guy' means leaving unsaid many assertive 'no' statements. These increasingly angry 'no's can build into a bomb of negativity inside which may, on occasion, explode, leaving them distressed, guilty and ashamed. Alternatively, the held-in aggression may seep out in bad moods, spiteful remarks or episodes of very bossy behaviour with subordinates or colleagues.

Although the Guardian personality has a lot of energy, they are quite nervous about taking risks. Security is a very high value for this personality type. It is second nature to them to play it safe. This originates in a concern regarding the disapproval of those in authority. Nevertheless, they are reliable and trustworthy, forming a steadfast and resilient backbone for organizational life.

Typically, Guardians are not adventurous or lateral in their thinking and planning. The concrete and the practical are their strong points. Their ability to implement, maintain and sustain what has been decided is of tremendous value. The Guardian types are particularly well-suited to managerial work.

Although they are good leadership material, the Guardian Good Father/Earth Mother can find it difficult to put themselves forward and so often miss out on promotions. They positively will not 'blow their own trumpet' or actively position themselves strategically. Moreover, they hold a negative attitude toward organizational politics. 'Politics is odious – it rots your soul' is frequently their stance.

Although very capable, they often avoid positions of leadership, preferring to be second in command. This is a real shame as their strong, realistic ego and their genuine care for others is much needed in positions of power and authority these days.

The Guardian Gifts

Reliability – They embrace responsibility with ease and competence. They take on tasks and complete them on time and to a good standard.

Human Warmth – People are comfortable and relaxed working for this manager. They feel understood and safe.

Resilience Under Pressure – They will stay with a project through difficult times. They will not lose focus when a task becomes unexciting (as Heroes tend to do). They are the great maintainers and sustainers of the managerial world.

The Guardian Shadow

Passively Aggressive – They can become stubborn, moody and belligerent. In extreme cases they may engage in provocative behaviours, producing angry reactions in others through covert means. They then judge the other's behaviour or 'justifiably' become angry in return.

Submissive to Authority – They can become self-deprecating, self-sacrificing and over-anxious to please those in power. Occasionally this may suddenly reverse and they turn rebellious. This is most often done covertly via mood and innuendo rather than straightforward challenge.

Explosive – Occasional outbursts result from pent-up anger. Sometimes these can be violent.

What the Guardian Brings

The feelings and opinions of others genuinely matter to these people. When their energetic system is not clogged up with unexpressed anger, their natural warmth and care enrich interpersonal relationships. Guardians are natural managers and characteristically feel at home with staff responsibilities.

Their predisposition to understand the other side of an argument eases difficult situations and builds bridges between individuals and departments. They have an enormous resource of energy and they are extremely practical and very realistic.

Limiting Attitudes of the Guardian

The Guardian attitudinal scenario revolves around notions of goodness and lovingness. These values explain many of the positive qualities so highly regarded in Guardian Good Father/Earth Mother managers. However, within the Guardian crucible, the definitions of both 'goodness' and 'love' stem from 'social propriety' rather than human depth and integrity. Goodness is often defined as being 'nice and polite' in these families and to be loving tends to mean you 'do not upset others'. Anger is seen as bad. There is an equivalence of anger with violence and a belief that the expression of anger destroys relationships.

Understandably, there is a deep binding of anger within the Guardian form. When anger is not expressed, it cools and mutates into negative moods and sulks where resentment, spite and hate abide. The experience of these feelings can be very upsetting for someone identified with love and goodness. This leads to stress and even depression.

Working through these misconceptions about anger and deepening the definitions of goodness and love are vital aspects of development and will be discussed in detail next.

Personal Development for the Guardian Good Father and Earth Mother

Mind Work: New Ideas about Anger and Love

For the Guardian Good Father/Earth Mother to expand into their full potential, there must be a release of blocked aggression. In this instance, because of the formative context, anger is a central issue. There is an unconscious resource of rightful anger about not being allowed to express themselves fully. Once contacted and made conscious, assertive energies may then be harnessed for positive, forthright movement in the world. The right to say 'no' directly even to those in authority will mitigate their typical silent and stubborn passive aggression. When explaining the Guardian personality in my classes, I ask the Guardian 'tribe' to cross their arms, look out at the rest of the class and say 'I won't and you can't make me'. They always laugh with delight at this playful mobilization of the power base in their personality.

In order to free up locked-away potential, core attitudes toward aggression must be reviewed and rendered more realistic. Most importantly, Guardian Earth Mothers and Good Fathers need to redefine 'good' to mean *truthful and honest* rather than *polite and nice*.

The classic management development positioning of 'assertion' as opposed to 'aggression' is not helpful here. In typical management speak, aggression is 'bad' and assertion is 'good'. I would like to suggest an alternative view.

As discussed previously 'gression' in Latin means 'movement' and various prefixes determine the nature of the movement: *pro*gression means to move forward, *re*gression means to move backward. The prefix 'ag' means 'toward'. So, *ag*gression in its original definition means to 'move toward', achieving what we want or expressing what we feel and think.

Because Guardians are uncomfortable about their passion and energy they easily buy into the popular negative definition of the term 'aggression'. Moreover, they typically interpret 'assertive' as meaning mild-mannered and 'nice' and hence fall into their own trap of blocking passion, refraining from speaking out their true opinions and reactions for fear of upsetting others.

Recalling the root meaning of 'aggression' discussed above helps us avoid this pejorative framing and instead stay close to psychology's definition.

Consider the possibility that aggression is a necessary and neutral force. Like any neutral force it can be used in both a positive and negative manner. A new and more helpful way for Guardians to think about 'aggression' is shown in the figure below showing 'aggression' as a neutral force that can be used in a positive or a negative manner.

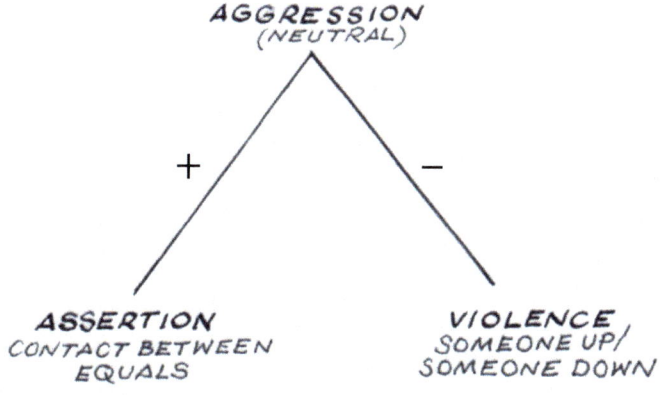

In this new frame 'violence' represents the negative mode of expressing aggressive energy, which, remember, is the energy 'to approach'. Violence is an extreme word and so it is not confusing in the way that the conventional 'assertion' vs 'aggression' framework can be. For example, I find that perfectly decent interactions get labelled with the pejorative 'aggressive' adjective simply because they are noisy or passionate, while low-key and lethal sarcasm slips through the net of criticism because it is subtle and quietly spoken.

In this alternative format, what differentiates a positive (assertive) comment from the negative (violent) exchange is not volume. It is intent. If we define assertion as 'contact between equals' and violence as 'someone putting someone else down' we have a more discerning lens through which to view interactions between people: one that is based upon interpersonal respect.

So long as our loud and passionate protagonist relates with the *respect* required when speaking to a human equal, s/he is being assertive not violent. The intent to make respectful (albeit not always conventionally 'polite') contact between equals defines the exchange in question as 'assertive'. Meanwhile, subtle sarcasm with its clear intent to do emotional or psychic harm that will undermine another's confidence or reputation is revealed as the 'violent' activity it surely is.

It is crucial that Guardians think about what happens in a psychological system when anger remains *unexpressed*. Organically, *we do not have a choice* whether anger ignites within us or not. Anger is a natural reaction that spontaneously occurs when we feel threatened or hurt. The *choice* we have is whether we express it or *hold* it *in*.

When *held in,* anger cools and then is recycled through the system. This 'resent' anger becomes 'resentment', which is in fact a low-grade form of hate. Resentment can degrade into more toxic forms such as aloof indifference or it can swell into vendetta and destructive revenge. The Guardian Good Father/Earth Mother identifies strongly with care and loving and so to find themselves in such states of negativity produces self-disapproval and stress.

The feeling we typically set in opposition to hate is of course love. A crucial and liberating shift in consciousness occurs when the Guardian Good Father/

Earth Mother realizes that in order to protect the love they have for another person they must speak out and process their feelings of anger and protest.

Guardians often confuse anger with violence. This is probably because they have themselves been violent (verbally and physically) when, finally, they can't *hold* accumulated anger *in* – out of expression – anymore. The ongoing, forthright and situation-appropriate expression of disagreement, anger and indignation is crucial to healthy relationships.

Body Work: Taking the lid off the suppressed power inside
Physical activity for the Guardian must be vigorous and full bodied. Power walking (taking big steps and swinging arms), rowing, swimming and gym sessions that lift and open the shoulders and free up the pelvis are all relevant and recommended.

The Guardian is full to the brim with passion and vitality which is *held in* by chronic tension in the shoulders and the pelvis. This brand of bodywork is like taking a cork out of a bottle of champagne. It is exciting and delicious.

The Mindful Management of the Guardian
A simple something that will make them relax: ACKNOWLEDGEMENT

These are people who like and deserve responsibility. Trust them with substantial tasks. They work well under pressure.

When they have done a good job, acknowledge it. They are so reliable and work so conscientiously that it is easy to take them for granted. Quite rightly, this will make them angry as, for one thing, your lack of 'thank you' is *rude*. Because of the block to straightforward assertion they will probably not tell you. Instead they may become demotivated and even moody or sulky as the anger cools into resentment.

Give them autonomy – don't interfere. Be a resource and a support. If you are the boss, you are 'the authority' and your backing and approval will be very important.

Never push or nag (Superheroes beware). This offends and the result will be passive aggression in the form of bad moods or 'I'll do it in my own time' mode. Remember, being told what to do and how to behave was the original wound. Once a bad mood has set in, be prepared to take time to talk the issue through. If you are not prepared to take time, leave it! A rush job on their offended feelings will make things worse. Usually, when you ask 'What's wrong?', the first response will be 'Nothing'. Take that at face value at your own risk (Heroes beware).

They get into trouble when direct confrontation is required. Remember, saying 'no' or doing something that upsets others is stressful. Many Guardian managers have had to break through this block to some extent but, nevertheless, it remains a strain. They may need support in a discipline situation or where they have to fight for their ground in a meeting. This difficulty will be less evident if they are fighting for others, for example, their team, the company or an individual whom they feel is being wrongly treated. Fighting for themselves is hard. It feels selfish! Encourage them to stand up for themselves.

The Guardian Good Father/Earth Mother often has an issue with authority. They may be compliant or in limited cases rebellious. Rebellion is really the flip side of compliance. The two look very different but are the same in that *what the other says is the stimulus for action.* If I am compliant I do what you say. If I am rebellious I do *not* do what you say. In both cases, what I do is determined by what *you say*. True expression and independence is centred in the self rather than in what another person says.

Crucially, they may not put themselves forward for promotion or leadership positions, so look carefully because they are worth considering. They are excellent leadership material. Once the assertion block is removed, the resources of natural decency and basic kindness along with reliability and realism will make them excellent leaders in these times of constant change.

In summary, the Guardian is an enormous resource of energy and responsibility. Manage them well so that all that resource remains positive and available.

Handling the Guardian Client

Behave properly. Treat them cordially. Respectful, polite human interaction is a key value with these grounded, hard-working, warm-hearted folk.

Be friendly. Guardians like to pass the time of day as people before getting down to business. This need not take a long time (unless you are a Hero type – a Warrior or Huntress may well think that 'Five minutes is a very long time!').

Guardians love good food and drink but they are typically too busy to take lunch on most occasions *but* be sure some sort of gastronomic hospitality passes between you on a regular basis. The core human rituals of sharing food and feelings are deeply valued by this type.

Approach with genuine interest in both work and private life. Remember personal events like the exam dramas of children or the worry of a sick parent. If these private details tend to slip out of your mind, write them down in your diary to refresh your memory when you meet. Remembering will count for a lot and forgetting can cost you dearly.

In all dealings be equitable, realistic and fair. They play by the rules. Guardians quite literally want to do 'good' business.

THE HEROES: The Warrior and the Huntress

This personality type is created around the Right to Love, which is formative between three and six years of age.

If sufficient energetic resources have cleared the previous hurdles of development, at this stage the child experiences a first romance. They literally fall in love with the opposite sex parent and in doing this they come into competition with the same sex parent. The emergence of this so-called 'Oedipal triangle' was the phase of development that Freud particularly focused upon when creating his groundbreaking theories.

This is a dynamic and delicate time where the quality of future intimate relationships and friendships along with a wholesome balance between work and private life are determined. Good parenting allows and lovingly supports the energetic and romantic unfolding of the child within clearly established boundaries.

The Developmental Crucible of the Hero

Somewhere between the ages of three and six, a fifth formative hurdle occurs. It is only when earlier needs and rights have been adequately met and respected, that the child moves into this Oedipal stage of development.

You may recall from your classical literature that Oedipus unwittingly married his mother and killed his father. Quite a tale of tragic passion and confusion. Freud gave this developmental stage that title because it marks the point where a nascent sexuality begins to unfold within the developing psychology of the child and romantic impulses naturally flow toward the opposite sex parent. At the same time an urge to compete with the same sex parent produces a dynamic triangle.

The more fortunate the child has been in terms of the environment's response to earlier needs and rights, the more fully committed s/he will be to the focus of this stage; that is the desirous and romantic feelings toward the opposite sex parent. A little girl asserting 'I am going to marry Daddy' or a boy saying to his father, 'Mummy belongs to me!' are typical stances of strong four- and five-year-olds, whether they are said out loud or silently planned.

At this point within the child's imagination, the opposite sex parent is like a numinous god or goddess and the feelings of this first romance are powerful, steadfast and devoted. I saw their impact in the touched and teary eyes of Sheila, my fellow trainer, when she returned to our classroom from a routine call home at the end of our teaching day. She had spoken to her five-year-old son Daniel who had virtually poured out his little-boy heart to her down the phone line. 'Mummy, Mummy when are you coming home? I love you so much and when I grow up I am going to marry you!'

Of course, there must be a rejection of this childish romance. Paradoxically, the right to love is established through a 'necessary no' to the romantic offer proffered by the healthily unfolding five-year-old. It is a poignant psychological truth that no child exits the formative years without significant and life-shaping pain. If life circumstances have been optimal and you have parented well throughout the previous stages, you must now deliver – explicitly or implicitly – a heartbreaking rejection. This 'no' is 'necessary' if your child is to grow into an adult capable of securing a loving life partner and sustaining genuine friendships with their own gender.

In the best case, the rejection is gentle and the heartbreak is softened, but rejection and heartbreak it is nevertheless. As we shall see shortly, parents who do not deliver the 'necessary no' and exploit this natural, childish romance, cause serious distortions within the consolidating personality.

Let's review: in an ideal situation, the infant has a good babyhood and enters toddlerhood feeling s/he owns the world. This omnipotence is pruned back but not overmuch so that the child remains spirited and passionately free. In such a case s/he moves into this last stage in full energetic flow only to get a devastating rejection.

The left brain is completely online at this point so the Oedipal child has a clear sense of self, s/he knows who s/he is and what s/he wants and how s/he plans to achieve success.

The thinking pattern of the Hero Warrior/Huntress reflects this psychological achievement. Thinking is now logical, rational and organized, reflecting the qualities of the left brain, which is now dominant.

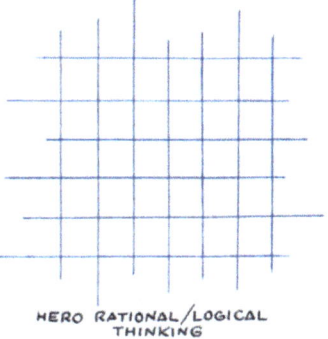

HERO RATIONAL/LOGICAL THINKING

In the best of all possible scenarios the opposite sex parent celebrates and supports the new emergent vitality in the child while at the same time affirming the relationship with their spouse. 'You are the most wonderful little boy in the world, but I can't marry you because I am already married to Daddy' is the perfect parental response whether said directly or indicated implicitly.

I CAN'T MARRY YOU. I'M MARRIED TO DADDY.

The child is gently but clearly rejected and so loses the competition with the same sex parent.

In this optimal situation, the rejection is definite but it is not humiliating and the heart is bruised but not devastated. The child relinquishes the romance and turns to their same sex parent to discover how to become someone who can *attract* somebody like the erstwhile object of desire. Ideally, the same sex parent is a good role model and so the child grows gracefully toward healthy adulthood.

However, even when this phase is handled perfectly, the body-mind shapes around heartbreak and hurt pride. In the body the pain of heartbreak is controlled through tension in the jaw (where crying begins muscularly) and across the chest (where the heart is hurting) and in the lower back where the pelvis is chronically pulled back to prevent hurt feelings from dropping into the belly where really deep sobs could occur.

"HOLDING BACK" THE EXPERIENCE OF HEARTBREAK

The Hero body is strong, symmetrical and athletic in appearance. Shoulders are square, posture is erect and there is a sense of dynamic physical energy and psychological confidence.

The jaw is square and may be jutting, embodying the feisty attitude of 'taking it on the chin'. The Hero jaw is fine and chiselled compared to the bolder often massive jaw of the Superhero.

Hero Warrior/Huntress eyes have a dynamic, intense look which challenges others in a direct, yet often friendly manner. The overall temperature of the gaze is cool, indicating the reliance on rationality, logic and the control of the feeling responses. In repose, the eyes often have a sad expression, reflecting the archaic and formative heartbreak.

Within the mind, the memory of the heartbreak that comes from 'giving your all' and being rejected is wired into the unconscious mind. The resulting attitude that typifies the Hero Warrior/Huntress is 'The worst thing in the world is to fail, and the worst failure is one where I look a fool'. Within the psychology of the Hero Warrior/Huntress any failure in adult life triggers the unconscious memory of this original heartbreak. This is why you can always count on the Hero type to finish a job and finish it well. So much is at risk within their inner world. From this same basis, they can become unconsciously driven to overwork and so put personal relationships at risk.

By the age of five the capacity to think and reason is fully in place and the Oedipal child defends against pain in far more articulate and focused ways compared to earlier personality forms. The protecting mind determines, 'I will never do *that* again. I will never *ask* for love. I will *earn* it instead.'

Typically, whatever the desired parent values will be the modality that this brave little up-and-coming Warrior or Huntress make their domain of excellence. 'If Mummy likes high achievement at school, then I will be the smartest boy in my class.' 'If Daddy loves sports, then I will be top girl in athletics.' 'If he loves pretty and cute, then I will be adorable.' Two differing aspects of the Hero type emerge in response to the parent who is impressed by the liveliness and beauty of the child and the parent who responds to rational and intellectual capacities. In the healthiest situation both aspects are supported and an individual of charm and responsibility emerges, along with that starkly requiring work ethic, which is a keynote of this personality.

By the way, in my classroom although some parents report Oedipal stories similar to those recounted above, many have no such experiences. In most cases, this triangular drama plays out subtly and below the radar of parental awareness, unless they are watching for it. The majority of my students are psychologically sound and in families like theirs such formative events unfold gently and effectively with wholesome results. Healthy parents do a 'good enough' job for the most part without thinking about it very much.

When this stage is handled well a strong, realistic and rational personality emerges with the available gifts listed below. The Hero Warrior/Huntress will be logical and fair minded as their thinking pattern suggests, but more guarded around the feelings of the heart than the Guardian Good Father/Earth Mother for reasons easily understood in the light of their history. When the 'necessary no' is delivered with love and respect a realistic and effective personality with a strong ego results. The ego image below reflects the psychological maturity and strength of this personality form.

It is clear that the Hero Warrior/Huntress ego form is very close to the ideal with its strong contour and appropriate size. There is no squelching down of the cutting edge of assertion as there is in the similarly strong and able Guardian Good Father/Earth Mother form. There is no block whatsoever to the assertion of the Hero personality type. They speak out and defend their rational principles with logic and passion.

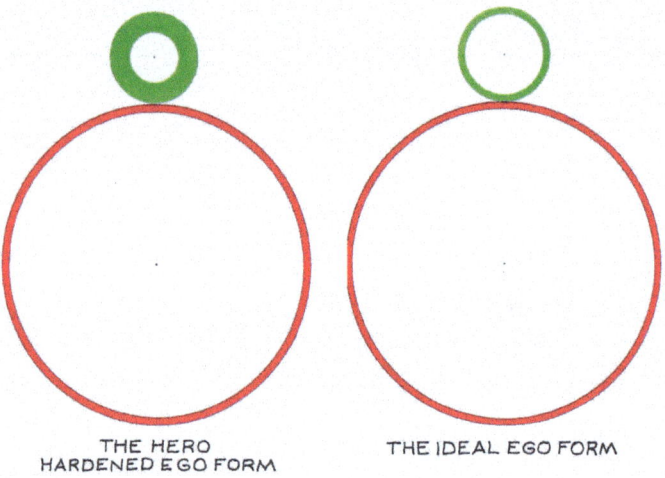

THE HERO
HARDENED EGO FORM

THE IDEAL EGO FORM

Where the Hero Warrior/Huntress ego form differs from the ideal is in the extra density of the line describing the ego. There is a hardness, even a rigidity, to the Hero ego that makes them less open to data from others in the external world and also from the inner world of the heart, the imagination and the deep SELF. Because they rely so greatly on their left brain capacities of logic and rationality, they tend to lose touch with their intuition and their emotional attunement, both of which are capacities of the right brain. Nevertheless, the Hero Warrior/Huntress ego and the thinking pattern that expresses it represents a developmental achievement of the highest order.

There are two ways things can go wrong at this stage, which produce two rather different and problematic versions of the Hero personality. However different they appear on the surface, the core issue of both is essentially the same: a defensive response to the question 'what do I do with my love and tender feelings?' Two mistakes in the formative scenarios produce two less balanced versions of the Hero personality. These two forms have the official – and typically ugly – names of 'histrionic' and 'compulsive' in the world of official psychology. I will use the more accessible and descriptive terms of 'the flirt' and 'the A student' respectively.

The Flirt

If an immature parent exploits the Oedipal event in order to feed their own vanity, the romantic flow in the child will become overwrought and hyper-activated. Imagine a couple at odds with one another and not getting along at all well. Suddenly this triangle erupts in their midst. An unhappy Daddy or Mummy might be tempted to respond to the child's numinous invitation to become a love 'god' or 'goddess'. Indeed, nothing less than 'divinity' describes what is attributed to the beloved parent in this situation. Remember that phone call my colleague Sheila had from her son Daniel?

If the couple's bond is weak and self-esteem is flagging in a psychologically immature parent, they may take up the offer and bond with the child against the spouse. The result is so sad. The child gets psychologically 'locked' into the parent and so may well become unable to make a commitment to an appropriate partner in adult life.

I worked for years with a beautiful and talented woman called Mary who could not make a successful partner relationship. All possible candidates were unconsciously compared to the godlike image of her father that she held in her unconscious mind. Her father, in taking up the infantile invitation to romance, had all but foreclosed her future possibility for a fulfilling partnership and marriage, because no real man will *ever* be able to match the glorious image of 'Daddy' as he appears to a little girl of six. In Mary's case, her father was right behind her, validating her view that no one was good enough for her. It was only after two hard years of 'examining her life' that Mary was able to let go of her illusions of a perfect partner, take distance from her controlling father and marry Jeff with whom she lives happily today.

The girl who 'wins' Daddy from Mummy because he has unresolved issues with his wife is not only at risk regarding her future relationships with men. She is also damaged in her capacity to be friends with women. Without the 'necessary no' the girl becomes fixated on the romance with Daddy and fails to make an intimate connection to her mother. A wholesome bond between daughter and mother creates a template for future female friendships. In this flawed situation other women remain competition rather than becoming intimates and confidantes.

Tragically, what 'wires up' in the little girl's brain is the excitement of taking a man away from his woman. This represents the psychological profile of the 'home wrecker'.

In adult life this way of being presents as over-excitable, coquettish and often seductive. Feelings are shallow and concentration is limited and quickly shifts from topic to topic. As outlined above, the histrionic Hero Warrior or Huntress is drawn to triangles. In these cases, the 'hunt' or the 'war' often concerns somebody else's husband or wife and victory is winning love that is inappropriate.

Much of the histrionic excitement is derived from breaking up a couple and so repeating the original scenario again and again. Workplace affairs are often based on this personality dynamic. At the same time, working relationships with same sex colleagues can lack collegial support and respect for obvious reasons.

In these circumstances the parents have failed to provide a safe environment where the natural emergence of romance and rivalry can be expressed and grounded.

Because the original scenario never arrives at the 'necessary no', the excitement of finding a partner gets fixated on the 'chase'. Others of the same sex remain competition, they are never friends. Once the battle is won or the hunt accomplished, interest often fades. Psychologically the histrionic flirt remains a charmingly lethal 'girl'. She did not have the modulating reconnection with her mother who would have ideally taught her how to be a 'woman'. This version of the Hero is more typical of women than men for obvious reasons, but we all know men who fit this profile.

In this personality, shallow emotions are used as a defence against authentic feelings. By exaggerating and theatrically acting out superficial feelings, the histrionic personality avoids emotional depth and the heart remains locked away and inaccessible. It is not unheard of for the true histrionic to become a manager but it is less likely, given the grounded concentration and common sense required for managerial work.

The A Student

The second version of the Hero form is referred to in psychology textbooks as 'compulsive'. When a sexually repressed, overly rational or shy parent is embarrassed or threatened by the child's natural Oedipal romance, they may respond in a shaming or punitive manner. The child concludes that this natural flow of potency is not safe and as a result excitement and feeling is resolutely controlled through thinking that is deeply organized and over committed and often based on doing the right (in this case logical) thing and never making a mistake.

I call this version of the Hero who always wants to get things right the 'A student'. The compulsive 'A student' form is often found in managerial work where their reality function and clear thinking is extremely prized. Moreover, they have the moral base to be good leaders, they are principled, dedicated to fairness and realistic. However, because they block their hearts, they may be unable to ignite and motivate others. A left brain is very necessary in planning and organizing, but people are never *inspired* by a rationale. It is a narrative – a storyline – that ignites feelings and fires inspiration.

Generally, the developmental challenge for the over-rational Hero Warrior/Huntress is to connect to their feelings so they are able to respond and speak from the heart. Given their psychological history we can see why this is difficult – but it is possible. Through the process of an 'examined life' attitudes can be made conscious and challenged. A student of mine wisely commented, 'You know you have a mind when you actively change it.'

Despite the wide differences in surface behaviour of these two versions of the Hero Warrior/Huntress, the energetic core is the same in both the histrionic 'flirt' and the compulsive 'A Student'. Deep heartfelt and sensual feelings are avoided either through *distraction* into shallow feelings (the flirt) or *contraction* into logical intellectuality (the A student). As with all of the other energetic holding types, the depth of the patterning is determined by the harshness of the original scenario. In turn, this dictates the degree to which workplace behaviour is influenced. An individual with a character style is much easier to deal with than someone with a more entrenched form that may on occasions reach a neurotic depth.

The Hero Warrior/Huntress Worldview

On the basis of a perceived reality, the Hero Warrior/Huntress ego concludes:

- *I am able and ready.*

- *Others are my competition and my benchmark.*

- *The world is a racetrack on which I will win!*

The Hero Warrior/Huntress at Work

This manager is self-sufficient, self-confident, competitive and ambitious. Like Guardians they are highly energetic and realistically focused on the task in hand. Compared to the Guardians, the Hero Warrior/Huntress is very direct and straightforward. Their main concern is to be fair, clear, logical and above all else to win. They do not worry overmuch about upsetting others or being nice or polite. Indeed, sometimes colleagues would like them to be more concerned for the feelings of others. Unlike the Guardians, Heroes have little difficulty saying 'no' and they can flare up with some temper in an argument. However, having done so, they do not hold a grudge and are quite surprised when they find that others do.

The Hero approaches life via their rational and logical thinking functions. This differentiates them from the intuitive Superhero and the feeling-based Guardians and the way they use their thinking is different from the Magicals and the Romantics. Typically, they are not particularly imaginative nor creative, nor do they enjoy ideation for its own sake. Like the Guardian, the Hero is an implementer rather than an originator. They are rational and logical and use these assets practically to get things done. Again, like the Guardian, they can be impatient with lateral thinkers if they do not deliver the goods on time to meet project deadlines.

Everything is a challenge to the Hero Warrior or Huntress. They set up endless competitions to keep themselves excited and motivated. 'I made it to work in forty minutes yesterday – can I do it in thirty-eight today?' would be a typical tactic to charge up for the day.

Success is everything and they can lose a sense of balance and move toward workaholic tendencies when pressure is on at work. Nevertheless, their goals of achievement remain realistic and healthy. They do not require themselves to produce perfection nor superhuman results. The Hero personality strives for excellence. Excellence is possible whereas being perfect or superhuman is not. Like a fine athlete who has run his or her personal best, they can take genuine satisfaction from having given the task their very best shot, even if it doesn't mean winning. Of course, they much prefer to win – very much.

This type hits trouble if they make a mistake or actually fail. Then their sense of reality wavers and they feel devastated far beyond what the actual situation warrants. In the face of failure or mistakes Guardian managers go immediately into damage limitation and plan for recovery. They remain realistic, thinking 'Mistakes happen. What can we learn from this? Let's roll with the punches of working life.' The Hero Warrior/Huntress lacks this realistic resilience to bounce back. Even talking about failure as a concept in a classroom situation makes them tense and want to go for lunch.

Because of this over-determined drive to win, this type can become inflexible and insensitive in their race to succeed. They often lose sight of people because of their over-focus on the goal. The reliance on cool intellect and logic at the expense of feeling and intuition can make a Hero colleague seem unapproachable, sometimes even cold, to those who work for and with them.

Gifts of the Hero
Achievement – They work hard and deliver excellent results.

Honesty and Fairness – You know where you stand with these people. They are straight and direct.

Rationality – Their thinking is realistic and logical. They are open to clear, grounded discussion.

The Hero Warrior/Huntress Shadow
Insensitive even Arrogant – Because of their deep fear of failure, they can lose track of the feelings of others and even force their logic onto others instead of giving them a say.

Rigid and Inflexible – They hate being wrong or making a mistake. They have very strong egos so they can argue their case relentlessly and without mercy.

Hard-driving – When they get overly task-orientated, they can push themselves too hard. They will then expect others to do the same.

What the Hero Brings

Like the Guardian, the Hero Warrior/Huntress manager is grounded and realistic. They are aware of the rules of daily life and they respect and uphold them. Unlike the Guardian, they are naturally assertive. They do not block anger and so are not given to moods, sulks or holding grudges as Guardians are. Although they can be over-reliant on logic and rationality, on the whole these are very necessary ingredients in the successful handling of the real world.

At their best, these are people of focus and courage. Because of their rational development they will challenge rules which Guardians may follow without question and so they are far less likely to get caught in a negative culture supported by questionable relational traditions. Heroes are dynamic and ambitious. They thrive on challenge and enjoy calculated risks. Their particular quality of goodness is a distinct and reliable sense of fair play. They want to win and will do their very best to achieve that goal but not at any cost, as is often the case with the Superhero. For the Hero Warrior/Huntress, the end of winning does not justify unfair means. Their forthrightness and their fairness make them valued colleagues.

The Hero's dynamic energy and their straightforward manner can be refreshing and motivating to many, but to less robust ego forms, their strong psychological presence can sometimes be daunting. It can be hard for Heroes to understand that their wholesome robust psychology can be a problem with some of those who look to them for leadership. Unlike the Guardian they often lack the emotional sensitivity that allows them to attune to others. The Mindful Management guidelines can be especially helpful to Heroes who want to better motivate team members.

The Hero Warrior/Huntress loves challenge. When the going gets tough the Hero mobilizes to make success happen. They are reliable and trustworthy and what they promise they deliver. Heroes are good leadership material, but the subtlety of organizational politics is a domain they typically disdain. Like the Guardian Good Father/Earth Mother, Heroes avoid this tricky arena typically insisting that 'Politics is a waste of time. I just want to get on with the task.'

It is a concern that the two moral reality-based personality forms frequently refuse to step onto the political field of play at work. I pose to them the question, 'If you do not step up, think about who will!'

Limiting Attitudes of the Hero

However well or badly the Oedipal issues are handled, the child forges distinctive attitudes within this crucible. They will be more or less entrenched or distorted depending on the way parents handle the poignant emergence of romance and rivalry.

'I'll show you' is a key reaction to the heartbreak of rejection. 'I will be the smartest, or the prettiest, or the fastest.' Whatever aspect the beloved parent values will become the goal of the emergent Hero ego. Success at whatever the task is seen to be becomes synonymous with being of value and worthy of love.

'The worst thing in the world is to fail' is a core attitude of this personality, and because of the early embarrassment around rejection that attitude is augmented by another related one which is 'The worst failure is one where I look a fool'. The Oedipal child unconsciously concludes that following the flow of feeling has led to the rejection and heartbreak and so 'deep feelings must be controlled and/or avoided' through either emotional shallowness or compulsive thinking. For the Hero, 'logic and rationality define reality'. In this way the high psychological achievement of logical thinking is used defensively.

This last attitude is less apparent in the histrionic variety but a strong and controlling mental function is typical even here. Behind that sexy, emotional smokescreen of attractiveness lies a strong controlling ego. Singer Madonna's stage personality embodies the archetypal form of the 'Siren' who hunts with her beauty. Moreover, as a businesswoman Madonna is as shrewd and organized as any CEO.

The archaic romance of the reason-able child of three to six was full-bodied in that it involved the heart and the newly emerged sexuality, and so new attitudes lodge at the base of the Hero mind which can cause difficulty with intimacy and commitment. They are 'I'll never fully trust a man' or 'I'll never give my all to a woman'. Because this 'heart and soul/sex' commitment is so total, the hurt is too much. As an unconsciously defensive strategy, Heroes may separate their heart from their sexuality by having partners of the opposite sex that they do not fancy and sexual partners that they do not particularly like. An extreme case of this kind of splitting would be the executive who has a wife at home and a mistress at work or in town.

Personal Development for the Hero Warrior/Huntress
Mind Work: New ideas about failure and success
A basic flaw in Hero thinking fuses personal value and being loveable with success. It is healthy to want to succeed but there is a driven quality in the Hero Warrior/Huntress form that is out of balance. Their will to achieve is over-determined. Hence they become insensitive and sometimes even harsh with others.

A sizeable shift required of Hero thinking is away from an over-reliance on logic and rationality in dealing with life. Frequently, emotion and intuition (the data from the right brain) are blocked and disregarded. If it does not make rational, logical sense, *it is not real*. A dear friend of mine who is a prime example of the Hero type confides, 'Warriors have an *irrational commitment* to rationality.' This is an excellent summary of the core issue of the Hero type and a perfect example of their cleverness and logic.

To be a successful manager and leader, this prioritization of the rational over the emotional must alter. Irrational qualities (right brain capacities) play a large part in human motivation and behaviour. Feeling and emotion are human fundamentals that are disregarded at a big cost. In their self-development the Hero Warrior/Huntress needs to become open to their own feeling resources so they can respond to the feelings of others.

In extreme cases Hero managers can seem heartless. This is very far from the truth. Heroes have deep and beautiful hearts, which they *guard* by locking a tension across their chests. This energetic block in the area of the heart reduces contact with their sensitive feeling capacity.

A major shift of consciousness occurs when the Hero learns that to *fail* is not 'the worst thing in the world'. However sad and bad they feel when they fail, there is something far sadder. The truly worst thing is to *leave one's potential unexpressed*.

I have known Hero Warriors and Huntresses refuse to engage in the domain of organizational politics, which is the doorway into high levels of leadership. 'Politics is a waste of time,' they say. 'I just want to get on with the task.' Organizational politics is an irrational game and its curvilinear hidden agendas and coded communications are intimidating territory for the straightforward and transparent Hero Warrior/Huntress. I suspect – and many admit – that they refuse to move toward more complex leadership opportunities for fear of failing. Playwright Samuel Beckett could have had these reluctant Heroes in mind, when he wrote: 'Ever tried. Ever failed. No matter. Try again. Fail again. Fail better.'

Body Work:
The body work for this type is unusual. Typically, they already incorporate physical fitness into their lives in the form of sport or exercise routines. For the Hero Warrior/Huntress, growing an awareness of the tight grip of their jaw and the lack of freedom of movement in the chest area is key. Loosening these chronic tensions through gentle stretching movements literally opens their sensitivity.

We often ask Heroes to practice letting their jaw relax and loosen while interacting with other delegates during our programmes. The Hero jaw is unconsciously held in a tight grip, so when they loosen it a little they experience themselves to be – as one delegate exclaimed – 'a slack-jawed git'. We encourage them to check in a mirror to see how normal and acceptable this change to a more softly held jaw actually appears.

The gripped jaw and the chest tension are linked. Softening the jaw relaxes the chest. With this subtle change in the body the Warrior/Huntress has more access to their own feelings as well as those of others. Moreover, colleagues feedback that they appear more approachable and open when actively softening this pattern of tension.

With increased access to their feeling capacity the Hero Warrior/Huntress can approach others respectfully and appropriately. Aided by the (somewhat) logical grid of the Centaur personality types, they can experiment with these devices to increase their emotional intelligence. Once the logical, rational Hero realizes *that feelings are part of the facts* of any situation they are on their way to transcending their limiting form.

The Mindful Management of the Hero
A simple something that will make them relax: ACHIEVEMENT

Challenge is the key to motivation in this type. The Hero Warrior/Huntress also likes pressure and far more risk than the Guardian Good Father/Earth Mother. Watch out for loss of concentration if the work gets boring. Unlike

Guardians – who often enjoy the ongoing nature of a task – Heroes can lose focus as challenge diminishes.

Watch for a workaholic mentality. Often the Hero Warrior/Huntress protects their heart by over-focusing on work. It will be a good investment for the company to encourage home time because dysfunction at work often comes as a result of the breakdown of relationships at home.

Being very independent, the Hero will not ask for support or encouragement. They are often embarrassed when praised, but deep inside they will appreciate the good feedback even if they brush it away with a 'That's what I get paid for' remark.

If they make a mistake, be *very* gentle. They will be giving themselves a dreadfully hard time for failing.

Help them to be more aware of others. Teach them that the task is not well done when their team or colleagues have hurt feelings and offended pride.

They usually need help understanding the political level at work. Superhero Wonder Women and Supermen, along with the Romantic Damsels and Poets are characteristically good at playing the game and do so often with narcissistic motivations and for the wrong reasons. The Hero, like the Guardian, typically disapproves of politics. They need to move beyond this rather adolescent attitude. Although both of these realistic types have excellent leadership promise, unless they embrace the political domain they will not reach their potential.

In summary, the Hero type is straightforward and uncomplicated to manage so long as you can make a logical case for what you require of them. They have a hard time respecting a manager who is not rational. The interface between the rational and logical Hero and the irrational intuitive Superhero is almost always difficult and painful.

Handling the Hero Client

Don't waste their time! Be rational, concise and exact, and above all else be prepared when you enter the precious world of their time schedule. You will need to be quick, to the point and energetic. Forget about being 'subtle'. Give them crystal-clear thinking that runs along logical lines. No curves, no fuzziness and no chance for misunderstanding.

It is a good idea to flag the hospitality ritual but saying 'We must have a proper lunch one day!' is usually enough. They would rather have a snack brought in so hours are not wasted in restaurants and, anyway, what do you talk about if the project papers are not in front of you?

They will appreciate you not taking up time with social niceties. By and large their private life is their own concern and yours is pretty irrelevant. The best strategy here is to talk the task, the whole task and nothing but the task. The one exception may well be a Hero Warrior or Huntress who is a new parent. They can fall totally in love with a new baby and then you can make deeper contact with them via a human approach to that natural joy. However, a new baby is not a guarantee of this change. So watch for tell-tale looks that say 'mind your own business', or 'stick to the point' when referring to anything personal.

Above all, be straight, logical and committed. That is what they like in others. Heroes are fair-minded, level-headed and despite their tough exterior, good-hearted people. With them you are in good hands.

Notes

1   Winnicott, D. (1981) *The Child, the Family and the Outside World* Harmondsworth, Middx: Pelican
2   Lowen, A. (1975) *Bioenergetics* New York: Penguin
3   Johnson, S. (1985) *Characterological Transformation* New York: W.W. Norton
4   Siegel, D. (2008) *The Neurobiology of We* Audio Book. Boulder: Sounds True
5   Schore, A. (2009) *Relational Trauma and the Developing Right Brain* New York: Academy of Sciences
6   Lowen, A. (1967) *The Betrayal of the Body* New York: Collier Books
7   Liedloff J. (1989) *The Continuum Concept*, page 8, New York: Arkana
8   Porges, S.W. (2017) *The Pocket Guide to the Polyvagal Theory: The transformative power of feeling safe* New York & London: Norton

CHAPTER THREE: Reflections

Metaphysics is concerned with the question 'What is there?' It constitutes the very first philosophical question and early answers addressed the nature of the world at large and of reality.

The metaphysics of leadership asks 'what is there' in terms of a leader. Centaur's answers are:

1. There is a positive principle within every person called the SELF, which seeks to guide us to the life we are meant to lead. This level of the SELF is based in natural ethics and human integrity. We urgently need leaders who access this resource within.

2. Inevitable wounding events in childhood caused each of us to build a protective 'body-mind' to ensure against being hurt again. This body-mind pattern forms the *unconscious* basis of our personality self – our 'way of being in the world'.

3. Although initially protective, the limiting attitudes of our personality keep us from feeling and then expressing our unique potential encoded in the deeper SELF within us.

4. When we 'examine' our lives, we can identify limiting attitudes and literally 'change our minds' and physically release chronic bodily tensions. As we free up our minds and our bodies we are able to bring more of our true potential to life and to leadership.

5. In order to embark on this inward adventure, we need faith in our true nature along with a map for the journey. Centaur provides both.

FAITH IN CURRENT TIMES

At the moment a kind of war between 'fact' and 'faith' is raging. A critical narrowing in thinking occurred at the beginning of the 20th century which led to the notion that we somehow have to choose either 'facts' or 'faith'. Two strong voices in our current mental atmosphere war with one another in a manner reminiscent of the old 'nature/nurture' debate that raged for decades around the question of 'what maketh man (and woman)?' Remember the conflict? Is it the genes we inherit from our parents that determine who we are or is it the social environment of our early years of life? Most of us have now moved away from the oppositional stance of 'either/or' on this topic into a more nuanced and evolved position of 'both/and'. The vast majority now agree that our embodied human reality is generated by *both* our nature *and* our nurture.

Can we make the same shift in our thinking regarding the 'fact vs faith' duality as we have with the 'nature vs nurture' debate? In one corner is fundamentalist religion, which is anti science and therefore typically 'anti fact' and in the opposite corner is what I will call fundamentalist science, which is flamboyantly secular and militantly 'anti faith'.

Fundamentalism in any form limits who we think we are and distorts how we live. Fundamentalism in religion arises from an over-investment in the dogma of any particular religion, leading to a denial of the validity of other faiths. Religious dogma has rather little real connection to the lived spiritual experience that ignites the start of a system of belief. Dogma is typically a set of rules and regulations constructed through (what we would today call) the 'left brains' of those who follow in the wake of inspiration and seek to institutionalize faith.

Fundamentalism in science arises from a similar over-investment in the function of the left brain typified – in this case – by an exclusive appetite for data generated through the scientific instrument of 'observation/hypothesis/testing/proof'. Just as fundamentalist religions deny the validity of other faiths on the basis of dogma, fundamentalist science denies the validity of alternative ways of exploring and defining the world. Through the lens of fundamentalist science, any view that is not based on (the dogma of) 'evidenced proof' is seen as unreal and invalid.

Proof and the Intuitive Outreach

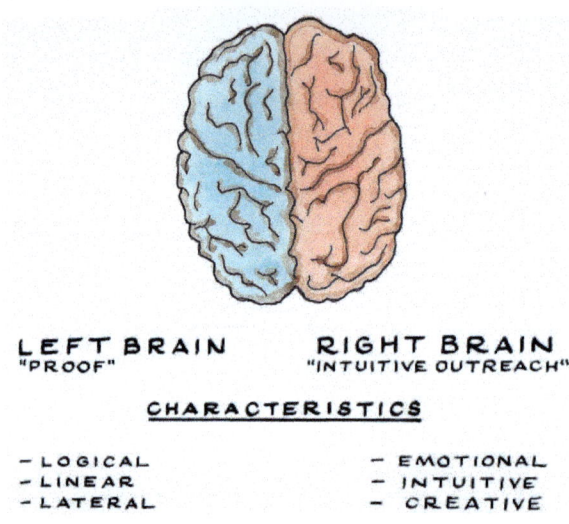

Huston Smith, philosopher and historian, helpfully differentiates two separate but equally important mental orientations which he names 'proof' and the 'intuitive outreach'. These two very different capacities arguably reflect what we know of left and right brain functioning respectively.[1]

'Proof' is based upon evidence gleaned through the left brain and a logical, scientific method of observation-hypothesis-testing. There can be no doubt about the extent to which humankind has benefited from this lens on life. From this base, statements about the nature of reality can be tested and proved or disproved on the basis of quantifiable evidence – thus producing a body of knowledge that is cumulative and can advance. The achievements made possible by science and its 'proofs' over the last three centuries are truly astounding: the overthrow of many diseases and the technological advances that gave rise to the Industrial Revolution are two of the most obvious.

Smith suggests that although the 'intuitive outreach' is utterly different in nature, it is of equal importance. Remember our discussion in Chapter One regarding a vast network of neurons identical to those found in the skull brain that are located in our intestines and around our hearts? You may recall that neuroscientists refer to these as 'parallel distributed processors' (PDPs). Neurobiologist Dan Siegel maintains that PDPs in the body have been shown to be able to process information in very complex ways. These networks of brain cells send information from deep within our bodies up into our right hemisphere where emotion and sensation may resolve imaginatively into an idea or an understanding *that is separate from conscious, logical deliberation.*

The outreach of intuition is not concerned with concrete data and proof, nor is it directed toward conquests within the *physical* realm like the development of antibiotics or the invention of amazing technologies. Rather than looking to organize and control our world through logic and reason, the intuitive outreach seeks patterns and pathways that provide us with meaning and direction as we live and struggle in this world as individual and emotional human beings.

Language – although primarily a product of the left and logical brain – also functions in the right hemisphere, but in a totally different manner. Language on the left is *literal*, describing objects in the external world with accuracy and precision. Within the right brain, the sensations and emotions of the gut and the heart resolve *poetically* into the language of symbol and metaphor. These have nothing to do with the pragmatic physical world of function and control. A metaphor or a symbol reaches for the larger – *metaphysical* – framework of an archetypal storyline or way of being or relating, within which daily experiences can be seen to have meaning, purpose and value. Such archetypal patterns provide guidance that can help individuals to live creatively amidst life's struggles and confusions.

Smith proposes that both 'proof' and 'intuition' are essential to human living. Each, he says, has a unique 'star quality'. Most importantly he maintains that they are complementary to one another rather than in conflict, representing two separate and equally crucial ways of connecting to life.[1]

The Rise of Scientific Fundamentalism

Early in the 20th century a number of scientists – inspired by a European movement called Logical Positivism – became fixated on the *method* of science, eventually coming to see it as the only valid way to look at all of life. As a result of this single-minded focus, the *instrument* of the scientific method (observation/hypothesis/testing/proof) morphed from a useful *approach to* the truth into a strict and narrow *definition of* truth. Anything that could not be evidenced and verified through the lens of the scientific method was considered false and illusionary. Proof trumped and intuition was discredited.

This 'scientific fundamentalism' grew out of the Enlightenment's Scientific Revolution but it betrayed the true nature of science in a most cardinal manner. The essence of science is its openness to new ideas and an orientating principle held dear is 'Never let the map become the territory'. When the 'map' – or instrument – of the scientific method came to determine and define the 'territory' of reality itself, scientific fundamentalism was born.

Professor Willard Quine – arguably the most influential scientist in America during the 20th century – proclaimed the basis of scientific fundamentalism resolutely in the following two principles:

> … there is fundamentally only one kind of entity in the world, and that is the kind studied by natural scientists – physical objects; and second, that there is only one kind of knowledge in the world, and it is the kind that natural scientists have.[1]

This exclusive focus on the physical – referred to as 'materialism' – is at the core of scientific fundamentalism. Materialism is the belief that the physical world is the only reality. Therefore, any concept of a non-material aspect of 'mind' (like feelings, meanings, values and ethics) as separate from the physical working of the 'brain' (swirls of biochemicals and snapping synapses) are dismissed as unscientific. A sound bite from medical materialism neatly captures this stance:

> 'If you can't cut it out it does not exist.'

To a large extent throughout the 20th century, intuitive thinking about value, meaning and purpose in life was relegated to the realm of the unreal and unimportant. So was any focus on ethics and morality. Thinking about who we are and how we might live with others went resolutely out of fashion. Such musings were labelled 'metaphysical', which was in no way a good thing to be.

This means that traditionally treasured aspects of the human mind like 'free will', 'inner authenticity', 'moral values' and 'natural ethics' are reduced to silly fantasies. According to evolutionary psychologist and materialist Richard Dawkins, we create these illusions as a defence against facing who we really are: totally biological creatures, in his view, with no purpose or meaning other than stark survival.[2]

In the same vein, Harvard professor Daniel Dennett – a high priest of scientific fundamentalism – boldly states that his professional goal is to usurp and destroy the traditional view of the human mind altogether and replace it with a materialist, reductionist alternative. Human beings, he says, are nothing more than 'a bag of chemicals'. We are 'big fancy robots' created through random accidents of evolution 'out of processes that are individually stupid and mindless and simple'. Within the worldview of fundamentalist materialism, there is no organizing principle of unfolding 'elegance' within the complex system that is a human being and there is most certainly not a deep SELF that guides our unique actualization.[3]

Dennett and Dawkins base their stance on a painfully narrow interpretation of Charles Darwin's idea of evolution through natural selection. Of course there can be no doubt regarding the validity of Darwin's robustly validated notion that evolution is propelled through emerging adaptations within species. Successful adaptations somehow better 'fit' the environmental context they find themselves in and so are 'naturally selected' to prosper. Individuals with adaptations that 'fit' survive and thrive, producing more offspring thereby shaping the future of that species.

But Dawkins and Dennett propose this process as the one and only cause of the cosmic trajectory from matter to life to consciousness. In their view all progress in human development is generated from a singular 'selfish gene' intent on survival alone. Dennett calls this 'Darwin's dangerous idea' and maintains that it is the best idea ever because it 'firmly grounds life in materialism' – the core tenet of scientific fundamentalism.

But Charles Darwin was not a fundamentalist. He was most certainly dedicated to the scientific method in his research, but he was not a fundamentalist materialist in his wider worldview. Darwin's connection to the *non-material* aspect of life is obvious in his reports of moments of wonder and spiritual delight that transcended the physical world even while he was in the midst of his concretely focused scientific research. He famously described such an instance of transcendent 'sublimity' when encountering primeval forests that are 'undefeated by the hand of man'.[4]

'No one,' he wrote, 'can stand in these solitudes unmoved and not feel that there is more in man than the mere breath of his body.'[4] Although Darwin worked from his (logical, linear and literal) left brain while he was gathering the 'proof' of his theory, he was also open to the sweep and wonder of an 'intuitive outreach' stimulated by the processes of his right brain.

Truly great scientists embrace *both* scientific facts *and* faith in the human spirit.

For Darwin, the physical world was a manifestation of a primary principle, which he was content to call God. Such respect for the transcendent alongside a rigorous study of the physical world using the scientific method characterizes the greatest scientific minds. For example, Isaac Newton, father of the Scientific Revolution, devoted vast amounts of time to his scientific research while at the same time dedicating himself to the study of the non-material and the alchemical. Moreover, Newton found nothing unusual in holding an interest in both of these dimensions of life.

Likewise, throughout his career Albert Einstein was a champion of both the science of the physical world and the wonder of the non-material world. He showed a palpable reverence for the non-material, maintaining that:

> The fairest thing we can experience is the mysterious knowledge of the existence of something we cannot penetrate, or the manifestations of the profoundest reason and of the most radiant beauty. It is this knowledge and this emotion that constitute the truly religious attitude. In this sense, and in this sense alone, I am a deeply religious man.[4 page 10]

A memory from his childhood evokes the enduring depth and power of the 'mysterious' and the transcendent in Einstein's imagination throughout his life.

> ... when I was a child of four or five... my father showed me a compass. This needle behaved in such a determined way and did not fit into the usual explanation of how the world works. That is that you must touch something to move it. I still remember now, or I believe that I remember, that this experience made a deep and lasting impression on me. *There must be something deeply hidden behind everything.* [italics mine][4 page 20]

All three of these great scientists – along with countless others – acknowledged and revered the territory of the imaginative and intuitive right brain, while furthering their science through the logical and rational left-brained instrument of the scientific method.

The Impact of Scientific Fundamentalism Today

Professor Mario Beauregard is an exception in that he is a contemporary neuroscientist who is not a materialist. However, he clarifies the current situation saying that, 'In their own minds many scientists in the 20th century have actually equated science with materialism and have come to believe the *purpose of science is in fact to prove the tenets of materialism.*'[5]

This identification of science itself with its fundamentalist aspect is dangerous – as we will explore – and it is having a damaging impact on how we think about ourselves and how we treat others.

Imagine that concrete, physical reality is all there is. That there is no higher or deeper power within us requiring ethical actions. What if we are silly or 'unscientific' to consider the existence of anything more than that which can be contacted through our five senses or their extensions in the instruments of science? Well, then we have conjured the shallow, one-dimensional world that legitimates the kind of ruthless and unethical behaviour which is having a terrible effect on our corporate community.

Cognitive psychologist Steven Pinker hails from the same materialist camp as Dennett and Dawkins. He writes about a current consensus of thought among neuroscientists – flagged by Beauregard – maintaining that '… the feature that neuroscientists find least controversial is the one that *many people outside the field find the most shocking* … the idea that our thoughts, sensations, joys and aches consist *entirely* of the physiological activity in the tissues of the brain …' [italics mine].[5]

Pinker scoffs at the intuitive and emotional (right brain) objection of 'many people outside the field' to such a diminished idea of who we are. From his view within the citadel of scientific fundamentalism, those of us who do not accept his basic, materialist view of the world are labelled 'unscientific' and therefore stupid.

In my experience, the effect of this atmosphere of dismissive judgment on the intuitive felt sense of human value is corrosive especially when it is presented as scientific fact.

Throughout the 20th century and into our present decade the impact of materialist fundamentalism has degraded our definition of our humanity and diminished what we expect from ourselves and one another. That includes what we expect of our leaders and also – maybe even more importantly – what leaders expect of themselves.

With peevish irritation Professor Pinkner questions, 'Why do people believe that there are dangerous implications to the idea that the mind is (exclusively) a product of the brain, that the brain is organized in part by the genome and that the genome was shaped by natural selection?'[5]

To my mind, there are dangerous implications to the reductionist ideology which proposes that only the physical is real and therefore all that matters. As philosopher Edward Craig points out, 'Our metaphysics – how we think things are – affects our ethics – what we think it is right to do.'[6]

And these days what some 'think it is right to do' is shocking and sickening in its lack of moral quality. Regarding the world at large, Jungian analyst and activist Clarissa Pinkola Estes writes:

> Ours is a time of almost daily astonishment and often righteous rage over the latest degradations of what matters most to civilized, visionary people… The lustre and hubris some have aspired to while endorsing acts so heinous against children, elders, everyday people, the poor, the unguarded, the helpless, is breathtaking.[9]

Within our corporate community, the conviction that 'the material is the only measure of reality', means that leaders wielding powerful influence are free to think of professional success as synonymous with a bonus number. Ruthless CEOs feel justified in seeing the 'bottom line' as the one and only arbiter of a good business decision and individuals confidently believe that it is okay to ignore the principles of ethical investing in order to grasp a personal fortune.

The belief that 'the material [money] is the only reality' has contributed greatly to our present worldwide political and social disaster. For example, in the legendary greed in corporate institutions, in the protection of institutional power, reputation and wealth at the cost of the innocent and vulnerable. And also in the legalistic claims of 'no wrong doing' voiced by embarrassed public officials in the midst of their various shades of shame. All reflect a worldview without depth and values. The stark atmosphere of these times highlighted by Estes is underlined in Mary Oliver's haunting poem 'Of The Empire'.

> *We will be known as a culture that feared death*
> *and adored power, that tried to vanquish insecurity*
> *for the few and cared little for the penury*
> *of the many. We will be known as a culture that taught*
> *and rewarded the amassing of things, that spoke*
> *little if at all about the quality of life for*
> *people (other people), for dogs, for rivers. All*
> *the world, in our eyes, they will say, was a*
> *commodity. And they will say that this structure*
> *was held together politically, which it was, and*
> *they will say also that our politics was no more*
> *than an apparatus to accommodate the feelings of*
> *the heart, and that the heart, in those days,*
> *was small, and hard, and full of meanness.*

Within the mental context of scientific fundamentalism, the intuitive heart of human life is denied and human capacities for spontaneous compassion and innate justice are dismissed as illusions.

WILLIAM JAMES AND THE SCIENTIFIC VALIDATION OF THE HUMAN SPIRIT

Just before the beginning of the 20th century, psychologist William James fulfilled a pledge made to his dying father by taking up a scientifically rigorous study of the nature of human spirituality. A medical scientist by training and a Pragmatist in his philosophy, James set about to discover whether there are any core principles that underpin all the conflicting creeds, dogmas and narratives of religions and belief systems.

James was not interested in any objective concept of 'God' as described in dogmas, creeds or laws. Instead he sought his data in the direct experience of spiritual vitality as it erupted into the subjective lives of individual – believing, doubting and praying – human beings. He wrote to a friend that he wished to 'defend "experience" against "philosophy" as being the real backbone of the world's religions.'

It is clear from the statement below, written to this same friend, that James held the various and conflicting religious doctrines in low regard. Creeds and dogmas, he maintained, are the product of (the left brains of) individuals determined to harden the spiritual into an institution. However, it is equally clear what tremendous importance he ascribed to the intuitive (right brain) 'felt sense' of his subjects' personal connection to their inner spirit.

> [I wish] to make the reader believe, what I myself invincibly do believe, that although all the special manifestations of religion may have been absurd (I mean its creeds and theories), yet the lie of it as a whole is *mankind's most important function*. [italics mine][7]

James sought his raw data from the widest variety of sources, with examples ranging from the primitive and grotesque to the most erudite and subtle encounter. His database was utterly massive and his recording and analysis robust.

He hypothesized, he observed, he recorded, and, in due course, he proved his hypothesis that: there are indeed unifying principles that underlie all spiritual traditions. Most fundamental was his finding that, despite vastly different experiences and interpretations, all subjects reported a *palpable sense of what they termed something 'more' than their singular and separate physical self.*

Of this wide variety of spiritual experiences studied, James wrote:

> They all agree that the 'more' really exists, though some of them hold it to exist in the shape of a personal god or gods, while others are satisfied to conceive it as a *stream of ideal tendency embedded in the eternal structure of the world.* [italics mine][7] page 554

This spectrum charted by James encompasses doctrines of belief from the most conventional to the truly bizarre. And, remarkably, it also embraces the scientifically secular yet transcendent third principle of Complexity Theory, which – you may recall – posits an organizing principle at the base of all complex systems that orientates them toward an ideal expression, which scientists term 'elegance'.

The differentiation offered by James regarding the nature of the 'more' shows that a person need not be conventionally religious in order to have faith in our human spirit. Complexity Theory's orientation toward 'elegance' and Einstein's notion of 'something deeply hidden behind everything' clearly belong to the latter, more abstract category where the 'more' is seen as an 'ideal tendency embedded in the eternal structure of the world.'

It is important to confirm that such a differentiation in no way diminishes the validity of conventional systems of belief. Religious historian Karen Armstrong writes:

'Many thousands of people find that the symbolism of the modern God works well for them: backed up by inspiring rituals and the discipline of living in a vibrant community, it has given them a sense of transcendent meaning. All the world's faiths insist that true spirituality must be expressed consistently in practical compassion, the ability to *feel with* the other. If a conventional idea of God *inspires empathy and respect for all others*, it is doing its job.' [italics mine][8]

Needless to say, fundamentalist versions of any religion fall short of the required 'empathy and respect of all others'. And so does fundamentalism in the domain of science.

Universal Principles that Define the Spiritual

James uncovered three core principles that hold for all experiences of the spiritual whether manifest in 'the shape of a personal god or gods … (or) as a stream of ideal tendency embedded in the eternal structure of the world.'

These are a belief:

1. That the visible world is *part* of a more spiritual universe from which it draws its chief significance.

2. That union or harmonious relation with that higher universe is our true end.

3. That prayer or inner communion with the spirit (of this higher universe) – be that spirit 'God' or 'Law' – is a process wherein work is really done,

and spiritual energy flows in and produces effects, psychological or material within the phenomenal world.'[7]

Taken personally, this final principle of 'prayer' both invites and requires a concentrated effort of self-examination in order to discern a deeper guidance – be it from a 'God' or an 'embedded ideal tendency' or a SELF – available to each of us as we live our lives every day. I suggest that this is the process of self-examination that Socrates said makes a life 'worth living'.

Such a deeper connection can be sought in conventional ways typical of organized religions where people pray together or separately as a ritual or a practice. However, there are other routes to such inner communion with something 'more' than our personality self.

Currently, the increasing popularity of 'mindfulness' in all of its various manifestations reflects a growing interest within the general population in what lies within. Modern mindfulness is a secular adaptation of an eastern spiritual system of cultivating an awareness of inner feelings and thoughts that promotes consciousness and grounded self-management. Many are finding their own unique ways of using these techniques to help them examine and deepen their lives beyond their limiting personality patterns and the disruptive emotions they evoke. Moreover, dedicated runners and devoted gardeners will know the impact that these non-religious – yet meditative – activities can have on fostering a connection to inner peace and tranquillity.*

In this regard, perhaps the greatest loss sustained under the sway of scientific fundamentalism is that thousands and thousands of people have bought into the idea that there is no point reaching for deeper resources of ethics and morality within themselves because they do not exist. I suggest that this loss of connection to our innate goodness has had a devastating impact on leadership in corporate life and the wider world.

From the perspective of fundamentalist materialism with its notion of a singular 'selfish gene', the ruthless and self-serving behaviours that discredit our corporate community *seem to be sanctioned*. Indeed, *if* the sole basis of

---

* James's research formed the body of the prestigious Gifford Lectures on Natural Religion, which he delivered at the University of Edinburgh. When published in 1902 in a volume entitled *Varieties of Religious Experience* it was an immediate bestseller and it remains a highly regarded classic to this day.

life is survival alone, *then* such behaviours logically follow. 'Greed is good' – the sound bite of the 1980s – reflects this worldview.

On the other hand, these same ruthless and self-serving behaviours have a different profile when evaluated within the framework of an 'ideal tendency' toward natural ethics that is embedded within every human being. It is from this other perspective that Estes's 'civilized and visionary people' respond with 'astonishment and often righteous rage'.

Within a context of 'innate morality', individuals who would slip away from responsibility – by maintaining (like Dawkins) that we are nothing more than animals or (like Dennett and Pinker) slaves to the workings of our physical brain – get placed firmly back on an 'ethical hook' where right actions are required.

Within this proposed 'metaphysics of leadership', errant corporate executives and others who abuse positions of power may be resolutely called to account both by those around them and – most importantly – by their own true nature.

So, Who *Do* You Think You Are?

There can be no doubt about the fact that our species evolved through the mechanism of natural selection. There is a fossil record that affords us scientific proof of the highest order. All that empirical science says regarding who we are is true. It is just not *all that is true*. The fact that spirit is not evidenced by science does not make it an unreality.

Absence of proof is not proof of absence.

Are you willing to consider the possibility that there is *more to you* than your familiar, everyday personality self and that this 'more' is a positive resource that can inspire a life deeply worth living? On this principle every one of the major religions' belief systems agree:

The three so-called Abrahamic religions – Judaism, Christianity and Islam – evolved their separate and differing creeds and rituals as they institutionalized the inspiration of their initiating prophets. Nevertheless, all are rooted in the Old Testament 'God of Abraham' who maintained the foundational conviction, proposed in Genesis, that human beings have a transcendent core.

'... God created man in his own image, in the image of God created he him; male and female created he them.' Genesis 2:27

However much dogma and doctrine separate these three (often warring) sibling religions, this principle is central to all: there is a spark (an aspect) of the divine in every one of us.

Likewise, Buddhism, in all its many forms, maintains that the luminous mind of the Buddha – 'Buddha nature' – is inherently present in *every sentient being*, and will shine forth when it is cleansed from what Buddhists call the 'defilements' – a good name, I think, for our limiting attitudes of mind. The word 'bud' literally means 'to awaken'. Through an 'examined life' each of us can *wake* up to a deeper and finer nature within.

In China a commitment to align to an 'ideal tendency embedded in the world' is aided by an ancient book of wisdom with origins as far back as the 10th century BCE. The *I Ching* is a divinational text used as a guide for moral decision-making as informed by both Taoism and Confucianism. As is the case with Buddhism, there is no central 'God' figure in these traditions. They are *nontheistic*. A questioner is helped to make contact with an ideal 'Great Man' present within human nature and, from that basis, to proceed through life in a balanced and mindful manner that serves both their own life and the larger world.

Hindu philosophy is the oldest of all these religions. And it is also often referred to as the 'first psychology'. The following verse from one of its ancient scriptures captures this universally central notion both succinctly and beautifully:

> *There is a light that shines beyond all things on Earth,*
> *beyond us all, beyond the heavens,*
> *beyond the highest, the very highest heavens.*
> *This is the radiant light that shines in the heart of man.*

(Chandogya Upanishad, 3.13.7)

Could this be the 'ideal tendency embedded in the nature of the world' uncovered in the research of William James? Is this Einstein's '...manifestations of the profoundest reason and of the most radiant beauty'? Is this the organizing principle that moves all complex systems toward scientific 'elegance'?

What if we put this notion at the heart of a metaphysics of leadership? What if a spark of the Divine, Buddha nature, the Great Man, this shining light, along with Plato's 'True, Good and Beautiful' are available within all of us and accessible through the 'examined life' recommended by Socrates?

WHAT CAN WE DO?

Having a model that proposes an innate moral aspect within is crucial to changing things. The first (and most important) principle of Centaur work is: *There is more to you than you think and it is positive.* Centaur further provides a simple picture that articulates different levels within our psychological structure along with suggestions as to how these layers interact with one another.

Whether we imagine connecting to something 'more' in terms of a 'God' or an 'Ideal Tendency' or through an image of a 'SELF' is a matter of personal taste. Jungian analyst Clarissa Pinkola Estes refers to anyone who is 'pledged to listen to a voice greater' as 'a believer'. And she has good advice about how to proceed in grounded and realistic ways within what can seem to be overwhelming times.

> Ours is not the task of fixing the entire world all at once, but of stretching out to mend the part of the world that is within our reach ... It is not given to us to know which acts or by whom, will cause the critical mass to tip toward an enduring good ... What is needed for dramatic change is an accumulation of acts, adding, adding to, adding more, continuing.

Estes continues with:

> One of the most calming and powerful actions you can do to intervene in a stormy world is to stand up and show your soul. Soul on deck shines like gold in dark times. The light of the soul throws sparks, can send up flares, build signal fires, causes proper matters to catch fire.[9]

As a Centaur executive coach I bear witness to small and important moments in this category. I find them both heartening and inspiring. Here are some examples:

A seasoned partner in a prestigious accountancy firm – let's call him Ian – changed the character of a meeting where snipes and sarcasm lacerated team spirit saying sharply: 'This is not how partners should be with each other!' thus calling up the archetype of 'Brotherhood', which is the symbolic basis of the partnership model. He spoke out in a moment of spontaneous outrage quite surprising himself as he did. In terms of Centaur personality type Ian is a Romantic Poet/Hero Warrior with a predominance of Romantic, so active assertion was not his strong suit. Ian's personal development work with me had been to explore his tendency to 'take the easy way out' of situations and his impromptu outburst signalled that quite some growth had occurred.

As astonished as Ian was by his own behaviour, he was even more amazed *by the reaction to his challenge.* Colleagues, having been 'called to account' from that deeper archetypal level, apologized and the meeting shifted in depth and moved forward in an atmosphere of mutual respect, leading to good outcomes.

In a second narrative that took place in this same firm featuring a Hero, a courageous personal assistant, whom I will call Sue, blew the whistle on her powerful and unscrupulous boss. And I am happy to report that the story continued in this vein of courageous 'right action' as the matter moved into the remit of the senior partner who is my client. Michael is a member of the executive board of his firm and is in charge of 'ethical affairs'. He takes issues of integrity seriously and regularly acts from a moral authenticity that is admired and trusted by his fellow partners. Michael's handling of this case was completely in line with his personal values and, to my mind, sets a standard that the corporate world would do well to follow.

Within the culture of the City of London, Michael's actions were exceptional, even radical. Typically, when a senior executive is dismissed for ethical issues, they resign quietly from their organization with their external reputation intact and then continue their career elsewhere with little difficulty. Michael refused this errant Superhero's resignation and insisted that his dismissal – based on a betrayal of the firm's ethical culture – be made visible within his professional community. In the wake of recent scandals, it is becoming fashionable for firms to advertise that they dismiss individuals on moral grounds. While the 'optics' of these actions are good for the firms, offenders do not really encounter substantial repercussion for their wrong actions. I am impressed and inspired by Michael's resolute commitment to call moral offenders to account. To my mind both Sue and Michael made their contribution to 'causing the critical mass to tip toward the enduring good.'

A Superhero in terms of personality, Sue's boss was turning in utterly flagrant expense claims *through her* to be processed by Sue's seniors and his peers and colleagues. Although those more senior to Sue pushed these claims back admonishing *her* for sending them in, *none of them* were willing to take the issue further through an established process of report. They were all afraid of this flamboyant and entitled Superman who was Sue's boss. Sue was not afraid. She was outraged and she made the wrongdoing known at the highest level. As a result of her courage, the errant and entitled banker was called to account and dismissed. Within a corrupted and also cowardly culture, Sue took a stand and – following the advice of Clarissa Pinkola Estes – sought to 'mend the part of the world what was within her reach'.

Speaking of goodness, one of my favourite stories unfolds around a Guardian HR director – we will name him David – who is also now a dear friend. By the time I began to work in David's company, these events had already become part of the 'mythology' of the organization, creating a culture of pride and safety within the workforce. Here is the tale: A young executive in his early thirties – shall we call him Joe? – became ill with cancer. The organization had excellent health care provision and Joe was duly supported through his rather long treatment, successfully overseen all the way by David's good Guardian heart. In due course he recovered his health.

Shortly after returning to work, Joe was headhunted and invited to take up a dream job in a rival company. He went to David and reported the offer, intending to turn it down out of respect for the care and support the company had afforded him. David took a totally different stance. He told Joe that the company had quite properly fulfilled a contractual duty and – while appreciating Joe's gratitude – he encouraged him to do what was right for his emerging career and take up the new opportunity. Joe was doubly grateful and in due course did exactly that.

David's generosity in interpreting company policy would be enough to get both David and the organization kudos with employees. However, our story does not stop there. Joe was a month into his new job when he was informed that he would have to have a full medical before being made permanent in his post. Alas this medical revealed that Joe's cancer had returned and the offer of the new position was withdrawn.

David heard of these events on the office grapevine and called Joe in for a meeting where he invited him to return to his previous position, which Joe – after some convincing – accepted. Joe then went into treatment once again and for a second time succeeded in defeating his disease, returning to work within months. Over the years Joe's fine contributions led to his progression up the leadership ladder within this splendid organization, strongly influenced by its HR Guardian. Recently Joe moved to another organization where he has taken up a very senior role.

It is no exaggeration to say that these events resolved into a kind of 'legend' within this organization, inspiring loyalty and pride which could never have been purchased with money.

I carry in my experience many such stories that illustrate how the light of a 'soul on deck' … 'throws sparks … (and) causes proper matters to catch fire.'[9] All of us need to know that individual actions make a difference. Goethe famously wrote a 'call to action' in this regard:

'Whatever you can do, or dream you can, begin it. Boldness has genius, power and magic in it.'

IN SUMMARY AND CONCLUSION

Let me keep distance, always, from those who say they have the answers.
Let me keep company always with those who say
'Look!' and laugh in astonishment, and bow their heads.

Mary Oliver

In the wake of Logical Positivism, bright thinkers led by Willard Quine made a mistake at the beginning of the last century that landed us with a limited and degraded portrait of human worth. That mistake, materialism, took a firm grip on popular thinking for more than a hundred years.

If it was a mistake, why did it have such longevity? I guess because the picture proposed was simple – in actuality *simplistic* – and, therefore, easy to understand.

Proponents could feel *effortlessly smart* and very sure of themselves. Above all they felt *in control*. It is human nature to crave certainty, and reducing the complexity of all reality to one level makes things both simple and certain. Moreover, the mode of living indicated by this view of humanity makes life 'easy' because all that matters is survival or – in corporate terms – profit.

Philosophical Pragmatism (favoured by William James) evaluates principles and beliefs on the basis of the practical outcomes they engender. Pragmatists actually name this tangible outcome the 'cash value' of an idea – this notion of costing provides a familiar language for corporate citizens. In this regard, the price we have paid under the influence of scientific fundamentalism is way too high.

We Are Approaching Moral Bankruptcy

The 'return on investment' of reductive materialism proves to be paltry. Plato's abiding values of the 'True', the 'Good' and the 'Beautiful' are set aside in order to make life 'simplistic', 'certain', and 'easy'.

It is time to reimagine who we think we are and to consider forming a deeper perspective on how we might live with others. In his millennial poem Ben Okri calls on all of us to 'snap out of' the trance or spell of materialism cast by scientific fundamentalists. In *An Anti-Spell for the 21st Century*, he invites us to upgrade and enrich our vision of who we are and so …

> *… pass from*
> *The illusion of our lesser selves*
> *To the reality of our greater selves*
> *… (moving)*
> *Into what we really are*
> *What we sometimes suspect we are*
> *What we glimpse we are when in love,*
> *Magnificent and mysterious beings*
> *Capable of creating civilizations*
> *Out of the wild lands of the earth*
> *And the dark places of our consciousness.*

It is time we placed the *physical* and material aspects of ourselves and our world within a larger *metaphysical* context of meaning and value. Within this expanded frame, life is complex and uncertain and we cannot delude ourselves that we are in control.

Yet might there be advantages in keeping company with those who welcome uncertainty and ambiguity? Can we imagine ourselves within the open-minded and open-hearted fellowship recommended in Mary Oliver's poem above? Would not Einstein, Darwin and Newton be among these, and Shakespeare, the Dalai Lama and that wonderful Jewish sage called Hillel, and also Immanuel Kant, Hegel, the Buddha, Jesus and Mohammed and, of course, Socrates – along with countless others who have related to life with wonder, delight and reverence?

We lost our way at the beginning of the 20th century when a *misappropriation* of the scientific method led to a *misreading* of reality and a *mistake* in our thinking about who we are. Huston Smith actually calls it an 'aberration'.

> This error triggered our disconnection from *the deepest belief that the majority of humankind* has always held about themselves: that we are creatures of meaning, purpose and value.

Although this severance has cost us dearly, it need not be terminal. As the gentle Huston Smith points out, since the cause of the rupture was a mistake, '… if we correct it we can rejoin the human race.'[1]

We are living in precarious times. Perhaps we have never been less in control. The impact of the recent wave of populism and individual, nationalistic self-interest around the world begs the question of how best to identify and achieve our hopes and aspirations for a better future. Centaur offers us a lens through which we might begin to build the foundations of a more authentic and fulfilling worldview, one leader at a time.

Over the past three decades, responses to these ideas within my Centaur coaching dialogues and my classroom teaching indicate to me that many of us are ready to come back on track. I think we are at a social, political and ethical crossroads and I believe we are yearning toward a right direction.

So, may I invite you – in the words of Alfred Lord Tennyson – to 'Come, my friends, it is not too late to build a better world.'

Notes

1. Smith, H. (1974) *The Forgotten Truth* New York: Harper Collins
2. Dawkins, R. (1989) *The Selfish Gene* New York: Oxford Univ. Press
3. Dennett, D. (1996) *Kinds of Minds: Toward an Understanding of Consciousness* New York: Basic Books
4. Tippett, K. (2010) *Einstein's God* London: Penguin
5. Beauregard, M. & O'Leary, D. (2007) *The Spiritual Brain* New York: Harper Collins
6. Craig, E. (2005) *A Brief History of Philosophy* Audio Book: AudioBook Ltd.
7. James, W. (2002) *The Varieties of Religious Experience* New York: The Modern Library
8. Armstrong, K. (2009) *The Case for God* pg 8. London: The Bodley Head
9. Estes, C.P. (2016) 'We Were Made for These' Times Internet Posting

Index

A student, the 169
acceptance 103
achievement 175
acknowledgement 159
aggression 113, 119, 156–9
amygdala, the 26, 30, 32, 35, 48, 50
anger 53, 57–9, 149, 156
anxiety 33, 37
applause 143
approval seeking 150–1
archetypes 66, 68–70, 73, 85
Armstrong, Karen 189
association, memory and 27–9
assumed reality 82, 90, 95–6
attention 107–13, 121–2
autonomic nervous system 49–50
awareness 123–4

Bastian, Adolf 65
Beauregard, Professor Mario 185
Beckett, Samuel 175
biochemical gender 79
Bioenergetics 46–7, 55–6, 73
birth
    order of 79
    traumatic 91
bitterness 117
Blumenthal, Heston 63
body work
    Guardians (Earth Mothers and Good Fathers) 159
    Heroes (Warriors and Huntresses) 175
    Magicals (Wizards and Sprites) 102–3
    Romantics (Damsels and Poets) 119–21
    Superheroes (Supermen and Wonder Women) 142–3
body-mind connection 43–60, 73, 80, 178
Bowlby, John 33, 34–5
brain, structure of 24–7, 30
    left and right brain 47–9, 180–1, 185, 188
Buddhism 192, 193

Campbell, Joseph 66
change, times of 67–8

characteristics, Complexity Theory 72–5

Characterological Transformation: The Hard Work Miracle (Johnson) 10–11

charisma 139

childhood 22–4, 26
- assumed reality 82, 90
- body-mind connection 43–60, 80, 178
- development of a worldview 22–4
- early formation of personality 60–75
- the five rights of the formative years 41–3
- growth rates 59
- Guardians (Earth Mothers and Good Fathers) 145–53
- Heroes (Warriors and Huntresses) 161–9
- Magicals (Wizards and Sprites) 87–95
- the nature of memory 27–32
- optimal frustration 82
- parenting 81–2
- Romantics (Damsels and Poets) 105–13
- and self-fulfilling prophecies 38–41
- Superheroes (Supermen and Wonder Women) 123–36
- the two kinds of memory 32–4

Christianity 191–2

clients, handling
- Guardians (Earth Mothers and Good Fathers) 160–1
- Heroes (Warriors and Huntresses) 176–7
- Magicals (Wizards and Sprites) 104–5
- Romantics (Damsels and Poets) 122–3
- Superheroes (Supermen and Wonder Women) 144–5

Collective Unconsciousness 64–71

competitiveness 170

Complexity Theory 19, 72–5, 188–9

concrete operational thinking 128

Confucianism 192

consciousness 37, 48

Craig, Edward 186

creativity 94, 95–6, 99–100, 103–4

cultural differences 79

Dante 67

Darwin, Charles 183–4

Dawkins, Richard 182, 183

deep self, the 63

Dennett, Daniel 183

depth 99, 100

destiny 62–4

development

    Guardians (Earth Mothers and Good Fathers) 145–61

    Heroes (Warriors and Huntresses) 161–77

    Magicals (Wizards and Sprites) 87–105

    Romantics (Damsels and Poets) 105–23

    Superheroes (Supermen and Wonder Women) 123–45

discipline 103

dogmas 179, 188

dominance 140

Duncan, Isadora 21

ego strength 71, 83, 134–5

Einstein, Albert 184, 192–3

elegance 74, 75

elemental ideas 65

emotions

    blocking 55–9

    expressed by the body 52–4

empathy 131, 135

energetic charges 107–8, 109, 114, 120–1

Estes, Clarissa Pinkola 186, 191, 193

'Ethic of Reciprocity' 2–4, 7

ethics

    definition of 1

    the Golden Rule 2–4, 7

    moral compass 62

    the SELF 6–8

excellence 171

existence, the right to 42

explicit memory 34–6

failure, fear of 173, 174

fairness 170, 171, 172

faith, in current times 179–93

fear, expressions of 53, 57

fear of annihilation 89

feelings *see* emotions

fight/flight mechanism 96

first adolescence 125

five rights, the 42–3, 87, 105, 124–37, 147–53, 161

flirt, the 167–8

formative years, the *see* childhood

freedom, the right to 42, 145–53

Freud, Sigmund 2

    dedicated to the 'left-brain' method 62

    the formative years 22–4

    Freudian-based psychology 64

    memory 23

    the Oedipal stage 162

personality and social interactions 5

the unconscious mind 21–2

fundamentalism 179, 181–7, 190

gender 79

gifts

    Guardians (Earth Mothers and Good Fathers) 155

    Heroes (Warriors and Huntresses) 171

    Magicals (Wizards and Sprites) 99

    Romantics (Damsels and Poets) 117

    Superheroes (Supermen and Wonder Women) 139–40

Golden Rule, the 2–4, 7

Guardians (Earth Mothers and Good Fathers) 9–10, 58–9, 75, 122, 138, 143

    childhood 145–53

    gifts 155

    handling clients 160–1

    limiting attitudes 156

    mindful management 159–60

    personal development 156–9

    physical features 149–50

    positive qualities 155–6

    shadows 155

    at work 153–5

    worldview 153

'gut feelings' 50

habitual responses 56–9

heartbreak 162–5, 173

Hegel, Georg Wilhelm Friedrich 6

hemispheres of the brain 27, 35, 47–9

Heroes (Warriors and Huntresses) 10, 12–19, 79, 122, 138, 143

    childhood 161–9

    gifts 171

    handling clients 176–7

    limiting attitudes of 173

    mindful management 175–6

    personal development 174–5

    physical attributes 164

    positive qualities 172

    shadows 171

    at work 170–1

    worldview 170

Hinduism 192

hippocampus, the 32, 34, 35, 36, 47

holding patterns 45–6

honesty 170, 171, 172

human spirituality 187–9

human warmth 153, 155

Hume, David 5

I Ching, the 192

implicit memory 32–4, 47

individuation 63, 66, 70, 74, 75

Inferno (Dante) 67

inflexibility 171

insensitivity 171

integrity 99, 100

intuition 135, 137, 141

intuitive outreach, the 180–1

Islam 191–2

James, William 187–9, 192, 197

Johnson, Stephen 10–11, 84, 110

joy, expression of 52

Judaism 191–2

Jung, Carl 2, 60–75
   the Collective Unconscious 64–71
   individuation 63, 66, 70, 74, 75
   Jungian psychotherapy 65
   the SELF 6, 61, 62–4, 70–1, 72–5

Kant, Immanuel 6

Klee, Paul 63

Kohut, Heinz 130

Kolk, Bessel van der 23, 47

language, development of 48, 181

Liedloff, Jean 90

limbic system 24, 25–6, 30, 32, 34, 86, 123

limiting attitudes 178
   Guardians (Earth Mothers and Good Fathers) 156
   Heroes (Warriors and Huntresses) 173
   Magicals (Wizards and Sprites) 100–1
   Romantics (Damsels and Poets) 118
   Superheroes (Supermen and Wonder Women) 141–2

Locke, John 5

Logical Positivism 181, 196

love, the right to 43, 161

Lowen, Alexander 45, 46, 89, 95, 113

Magicals (Wizards and Sprites) 9, 18–19, 33, 39–41, 57, 138
   babyhood 87–95
   gifts 99
   handling clients 104–5
   limiting attitudes 100–1
   Mindful Management 103–4
   personal development 101–3
   physical attributes 92–3, 95
   positive qualities 99–100
   shadows 99

at work 95–8
mammalian brain, the 25
materialism 182, 185, 196–7
materialist fundamentalism 186–7
maternal bonding 93
memory 23, 26
  explicit memory 34–6
  implicit memory 32–4, 47
  the nature of 27–32
  and self-fulfilling prophecies 38–41
  the structure of the brain and 24–7
  transference 37
metaphysics, definition of 1
Meyers-Briggs Type Indicator (MBTI) test 77
midlife crises 67–8
mind work
  Guardians (Earth Mothers and Good Fathers) 156–9
  Heroes (Warriors and Huntresses) 174–5
  Magicals (Wizards and Sprites) 101–2
  Romantics (Damsels and Poets) 118–19
  Superheroes (Supermen and Wonder Women) 142
mindful management 20
  Guardians (Earth Mothers and Good Fathers) 159–60
  Heroes (Warriors and Huntresses) 175–6
  Magical (Wizards and Sprites) 103–4
  Romantics (Damsels and Poets) 121–2
  Superheroes (Supermen and Wonder Women) 143–4
mindfulness 190
mirroring 129
moral compass 62
muscular system, the 50

'nature and nurture' 78
neocortex, the 26–7, 35, 48
networking 116
neurology 23–4
neuroscience 43–60, 86, 123, 125, 180–1
  autonomic nervous system 49–50
  Bioenergetics 46–7
  body-mind connection 43–60, 50–60
  the Complexity Theory 19, 72–5
  holding patterns 45–6
  left and right brain 47–9
Newton, Isaac 184
nourishment, the right to 42, 105

Obama, President Barack 117
objectification of others 132
Odyssey (Homer) 67
Oedipal stage 161–9
Okri, Ben 197
Oliver, Mary 187, 196
opportunistic thinking 126
optimal frustration 82

parallel-distributed processors (PDPs) 50, 180
paranoia 93, 104, 105
parasympathetic system 50
parenting 81–2
passive aggression 151, 154, 155
perception 29, 30, 37
perfectionism 96, 101, 133
personal development
    Guardians (Earth Mothers and Good Fathers) 156–9
    Heroes (Warriors and Huntresses) 174–5
    Magicals (Wizards and Sprites) 101–3
    Romantics (Damsels and Poets) 118–21
    Superheroes (Supermen and Wonder Women) 142–3
personal trainers 121–2
personality
    creation of 8
    early formation of 60–75
    social interactions and 5–6
    transformational changes in 10–11
personality self, the 63
personality types
    archetypes 66, 68–70, 73, 85
    Guardians (Earth Mothers and Good Fathers) 9–10, 14–15, 58–9, 75, 122, 138, 143, 145–61
    Heroes (Warriors and Huntresses) 10, 12–19, 79, 122, 138, 143, 161–77
    holding patterns 45–6
    Magicals (Wizards and Sprites) 9, 18–19, 33, 39–41, 57, 87–105, 138
    Romantics (Damsels and Poets) 9, 16–18, 33, 105–23, 138
    Superheroes (Supermen and Wonder Women) 9, 15–16, 123–45
perspectives 77–83
Philosophical Pragmatism 197
physical attributes
    Guardians (Earth Mothers and Good Fathers) 149–50
    Heroes (Warriors and Huntresses) 164
    Magicals (Wizards and

Sprites) 92–3, 95
    Romantics (Damsels and Poets) 113
    Superheroes (Supermen and Wonder Women) 135–6
Pierrakos, John 45, 46
Pinker, Steven 185–6
Plato 6, 62, 193, 197
playfulness 117
populism, in politics 1
positive qualities
    Guardians (Earth Mothers and Good Fathers) 155–6
    Heroes (Warriors and Huntresses) 172
    Magicals (Wizards and Sprites) 99–100
    Romantics (Damsels and Poets) 117
    Superheroes (Supermen and Wonder Women) 140–1
potential 78
power, the right to 42, 124–37
presentations 116
pressure 103
priming 30
promotion 104
proof 180
psychology, three basic notions 81–3

Quine, Professor Willard 182, 196

rationality 170, 171, 172, 174
reality, assumed 82, 90, 95–6
reality function 130–7
Reich, William 2, 43–4, 46–7, 50–60, 73
rejection 88–90, 100–1
relaxation 117
reliability 153, 154, 155
religion 191–3
    the Golden Rule in 3–4
    and the SELF 6–7
reptilian brain, the 25
resentment 158
resilience under pressure 155
respect
    differences in perception 11–19
    importance of 7
Right to Exist 42, 87
Right to Freedom 42, 145–53
Right to Love 43, 161
Right to Nourishment 42, 105
Right to Power 42, 124–37
rigidness 171
Romantics (Damsels and Poets) 9, 16–18, 33, 138
    babyhood 105–13
    gifts 117

handling clients 122–3

limiting attitudes 118

Mindful Management 121–2

personal development 118–21

physical attributes 113

positive qualities 117

shadows 117

at work 114–17

worldview 113

Rumi 38

ruthlessness 140

sadness, expression of 52

scheming 140

Schore, Allan 23, 86

scientific fundamentalism 181–7, 190

Scientific Revolution, the 182, 184

seat of emotions, the 25

SELF, the 6–8, 61, 62–4, 70–1, 72–5, 134–5, 137, 141, 142, 148, 178, 190, 193

self-assertion, lack of 147, 150, 153–5, 157, 160

self-confidence 102

self-fulfilling prophecies 38–41

sensitivity 117

shadows

    Guardians (Earth Mothers and Good Fathers) 155

    Heroes (Warriors and Huntresses) 171

    Magicals (Wizards and Sprites) 99

    Romantics (Damsels and Poets) 117

    Superheroes (Supermen and Wonder Women) 140

Siegel, Daniel 30, 86

    body-mind connection 47

    on the Complexity Theory 72, 74

    the left and right brain 48, 49

    memory 22, 23, 32

    the need for social interactions 25

    parallel-distributed processors (PDPs) 180

Smith, Huston 180, 181, 198

social interactions, personality and 5–6

Socrates 6, 7, 31, 61, 71, 190

soma reading 34, 51, 55–6

Spark of the Divine 62

spirituality 187–91

strategic thinking 137, 140, 144

subliminal triggering 30

success, importance of 170

Superheroes (Supermen and Wonder Women) 9, 15–16

    gifts 139–40

handling clients 144–5
limiting attitudes 141–2
mindful management 143–4
personal development 142–3
physical features 135–6
positive qualities 140–1
shadows 140
toddlerhood 123–36
at work 137–9
worldview 137
sympathetic system 49

Taoism 192
temperament 77–83, 106, 127
Tennyson, Alfred Lord 198
tension 112–13
theory of other minds, the 130–7
transformational changes 10–11, 67–8
traumatic birth 91

unconscious mind, the 21–4
assumed reality 82, 90, 95–6
body-mind connection 43–60, 80, 178
Collective Unconsciousness 64–71
the five rights of the formative years 41–3
the nature of memory 27–32

optimal frustration 82
parenting 81–2
and self-fulfilling prophecies 38–41
two kinds of memory 32–4
universal principles, spirituality 189–90

violence 99, 155, 158, 159

Winnicott, Donald 81
withdrawal 99
workplace
Guardians (Earth Mothers and Good Fathers) 153–5
Heroes (Warriors and Huntresses) 170–1
Magicals (Wizards and Sprites) 95–8
Romantics (Damsels and Poets) 114–17
Superheroes (Supermen and Wonder Women) 137–9
worldview
assumed reality 82, 90, 95–6
body-mind connection 43–60
early formation of personality 60–75
establishment of 21–4, 26
the five rights of the formative years 41–3

Guardians (Earth Mothers and Good Fathers) 153

Heroes (Warriors and Huntresses) 170

Magicals (Wizards and Sprites) 87–95

the nature of memory 27–32

optimal frustration 82

parenting 81–2

Romantics (Damsels and Poets) 113

scientific fundamentalism 181–7

and self-fulfilling prophecies 38–41

Superheroes (Supermen and Wonder Women) 137

temperament and 77–83

two kinds of memory 32–4

NOTES

NOTES

NOTES

NOTES